1 Lutheran Church
3 Catholic
9 M.C.R.R. Depot
10 Cemetery
11 Fair Ground
12 Oil Well
13 Murry & Finley
14 C.C. Wells Planing Mills
15 D. & W. Knapp Flouring Mills
16 J. M. Hall & Co. Flour Mills
17 Rothmaster Flour Mills

NTY, MICHIGAN

Niles, the city of Four Flags, has a rich culture and tradition. It is on the long history that the future of Niles can be built. We at Old Kent Bank-Southwest have sponsored this pictorial history because we are happy to be a part of that past and are optimistic about the future.

Not only is Old Kent Bank-Southwest, as a financial institution, a part of this community, but also our Directors, Officers and Staff share in the life of this community as residents. We share with you the past of Niles and will work with you in building the future.

Old Kent Bank-Southwest wishes to dedicate this book to the citizens of Niles, past and present, whose faith, courage and determination have helped to build a strong foundation for our city's progress and growth.

James W. Giffin

James W. Giffin

Chairman, President & CEO

TRICENTENNIAL EDITION

Niles, Michigan

A PICTORIAL HISTORY

by
D. Wayne Stiles
Nancy Watts-Stiles

G. BRADLEY PUBLISHING, INC.
ST. LOUIS, MO

Niles, Michigan
A PICTORIAL HISTORY

By
D. Wayne Stiles
Nancy Watts-Stiles

A limited edition of 2,000
of which this is...

669

Publication Staff:
Authors: D. Wayne Stiles
              Nancy Watts-Stiles
Cover Artist: William Blackmun
Book Design: Diane Kramer
Publisher: G. Bradley Publishing, Inc.
Sponsor: Old Kent Bank-Southwest

Copyright 1991 by G. Bradley Publishing, Inc. All rights reserved. Printed in the United States of America. No part of this publication may be reproduced, stored in a retrieval system, or transmitted, in any form or by any means, electronic, mechanical, photocopying, recording or otherwise, without the prior permission of the publisher.

ISBN 0-943963-18-4
Printed in the United States of America

Table of Contents

Foreword 6

Chapter I: 1691-1829, The Colonial Era 7

Chapter II: 1829-1848, Pioneers & Progress 29

Chapter III: 1848-1890, Era of Transition 43

Chapter IV: 1890-1950, Growth and Prosperity 129

Chapter V: 1950-Present, The Modern Era.......................177

Acknowledgements 196

Bibliography..197

Contributors..197

Index..198

FOREWORD

Three hundred years ago, in the summer of 1691, a young French officer, Augustine LeGardeur de Courtemanche, and his men arrived here in the peaceful valley of the river we know as the Saint Joseph. They were under orders of the French government to establish an official French military outpost here where the Sauk Trail crossed the river. The fort they built, the little village which grew up around it, and the river itself, came to be called Saint Joseph after the nearby mission station of the Jesuit missionaries.

Thus began our community's 300 year voyage to the present. Since that genesis the community has been claimed by four sovereign nations. Four flags have flown over it, the national banners of France, England, Spain, and the United States, not to mention the emblems and totems of the native Americans, the Miami and Potawatomi.

By virtue of its location on the river and trails, the Fort Saint Joseph area became a center for trade — European made goods in exchange for the products of the forests and the fields. As the years passed and the flags changed, the community became the City of Niles. First the riverboats, then the railroads came to serve the town. They brought not only commerce and prosperity, but also the emigrants of the many ethnic and national origins from whom most of us are descended.

It is also because of our location in the nation's heartland, with good rail and water connections, that Niles can boast of the large, locally owned industries which have called it home. Among them, National Standard, Simplicity Pattern, Garden City Fan, Tyler Refrigeration, French Paper, and Kawneer, to name a few.

History records that a number of people have been reared in Niles who have had a profound effect, not only on the City of Niles, but also on the nation as well. Niles was the boyhood home of such notables as Montgomery Ward (the originator of mail order sales), John and Horace Dodge (automobile pioneers), Ring Lardner (author, columnist, and humorist), Vic Hyde (entertainer), and Dr. Fred Bonine (the famous eye surgeon).

As citizens of Niles, we can reflect with pride in this Tri-Centennial year on our rich heritage and we can acknowledge with respect those who have gone before us. Like other communities, we too have suffered the rigors of many wars; we too have endured the hardships of recession and depression; but through them all we have prospered as a community because of the sacrifices of previous generations.

In this 1991 Tri-Centennial year we must therefore rededicate ourselves to working together for the common good, and to prepare for any sacrifices necessary to insure that the generations as yet unborn will have a positive and prosperous City of Niles in which to live and flourish.

Larry W. Clymer
Mayor
City of Niles

Chapter I

1691-1829

The Colonial Era

First there was the river. The native Americans called it the "Sa-wa-see-be" or variations of that name. For centuries the river shallows located in present-day Niles provided a place where men carrying packs on their backs could wade across it as they followed The Great Sauk Trail. This ancient trade route stretched from the Mississippi to the present-day cities of Montreal and Quebec. Before the arrival of the Europeans in the 1500's, there had been trade between the tribes in tool-making flint and native copper, animal skins for warm robes and garments, as well as food items such as corn, beans, squash, wild rice, maple sugar, and tobacco.

In 1679 the explorer La Salle, (whose expedition was the first known to have visited this area) followed routes long known to his Indian guides and their forefathers. La Salle and his men camped at the mouth of the river where it flows into Lake Michigan while they waited futilely for the arrival of their supply vessel, the *Griffin*. They were unaware that it had become the first sailing ship to be lost on the Great Lakes. They waited nearly a month for the arrival of the ship and for the rest of the exploration party to catch up with them. To protect their camp from the overwhelmingly friendly Indians and to keep the idle and mutinous explorers busy, he put the men to work erecting a temporary palisade about their quarters. This "make work project" kept the men occupied until La Salle decided to give up the wait for the *Griffin* and continue the expedition. When the group resumed their explorations they traveled up the river toward the portage which connected the St. Joseph River with the Kankakee River which leads to the Mississippi. Upstream some sixty leagues (about 65 miles from Lake Michigan) they passed the place where the major cross-country Indian trade route, the Great Sauk Trail, crossed the river. This strategic location was soon to become the site of the French community known as Fort Saint Joseph.

In the early 1680's, the Jesuit missionaries recognized the critical importance of this location. Father Jean-Claude Allouez established a mission station and named it Saint Joseph de la Miami in honor of their patron, Saint Joseph. At that time the predominant tribe in the area was the Miami, though members of a number of different tribes could be found in the general locale.

In 1689 a major attack on French Canada was made by the powerful and belligerent Iroquois confederation of tribes who were firmly aligned with the British interests in North America. As a result of this attack, the faith of France's own Indian allies was seriously shaken, even though the attacks were beaten off. In an effort to "show the flag to the Indians" and restore their confidence in the French, a fort was authorized near the Mission of Saint Joseph on the

A painting of Sieur de La Salle in front of Louis XIV and Colbert at Versailles by d'Adrien Moreau in the Chateau Ramezay in Montreal. La Salle made several trips back to the French court at Versailles to obtain permission for his explorations. Here he is illustrated bowing before the king (in the hat) and the prime minister.

Jesuit priests founded the mission. Many came from France but some were trained at seminaries in Canada.

River of the Miamis. It was built and manned in 1691 by soldiers of the French Colonial Army (known as *Troupes de la Marine*), under the leadership of Augustine Legardeur de Courtemanche, by order of Governor General Frontenac. The construction of Fort Saint Joseph marks the beginning of the first permanent European community in lower Michigan, if not the entire state.

While documents describing the early French fort in exact detail have yet to be located, it is safe to assume that it was typical of the outposts planted by the French in the interior of North America. If so, it was rectangular in shape with small bastions at each corner. Contained within the palisade walls would be several buildings built by setting logs in the ground in the same manner as the palisade. The cracks between these posts, which formed the walls, were stuffed with a mixture of clay and grass. The roofs were made of bark or thatched with grass. This method of building (called *poteaux en terre* or post-in-ground) was common in French Colonial North America.

The buildings within the palisade would have housed the officers and the men as well as storage buildings for the trade goods. Trading would have been conducted at a trading building or the ranking officer's residence. As the outpost grew in population, additional buildings would have been built outside the palisaded fort for civilian traders and for the married soldiers who lived "off post."

Later descriptions make it clear that Fort Saint Joseph was built for strategic rather than tactical purposes. It was built on the banks of the river rather than on the bluffs which overlooked it. In its nearly 100 years of existence, the fort's primary function was to provide a secure location for the exchange of manufactured goods from Europe for the natural and fur products gathered by the local native Americans. This exchange or trade was the basis of the friendly rela-

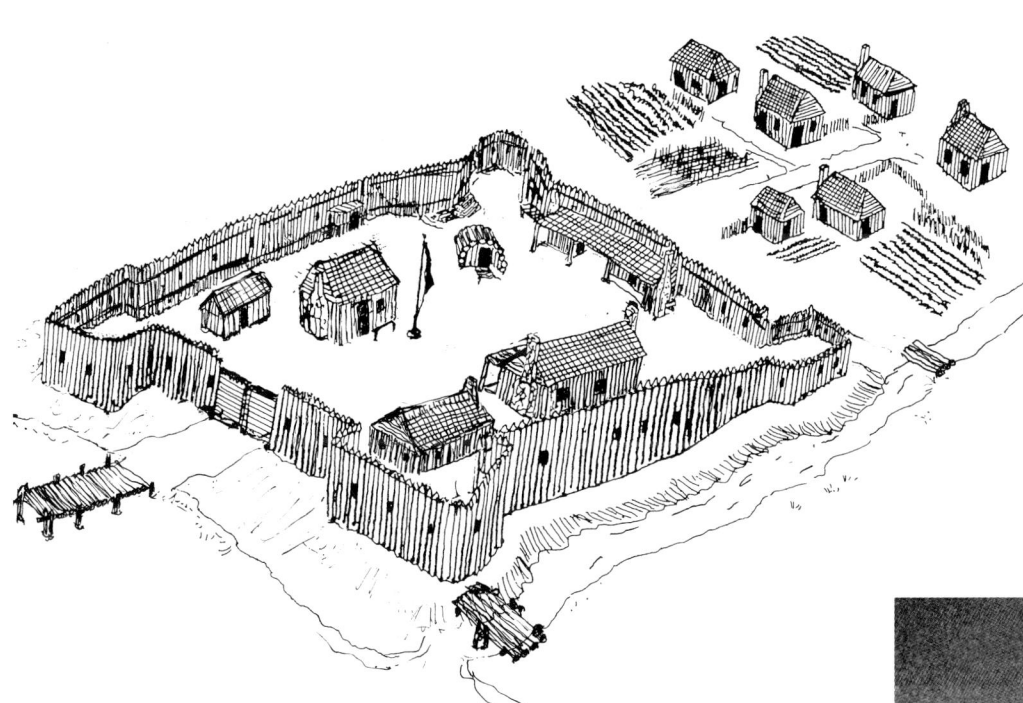

An artist's interpretation of a typical French fur trading fort showing the beginning of a civilian community outside the palisade walls. This is probably quite similar to the way Fort Saint Joseph would have looked in the 1720's.

This *poteaux en terre* style row house is part of the reconstruction at Fort Michillimakinac. Houses at Fort Saint Joseph were probably built this way.

tionship between the local Indians and the French.

In the early years these trade items were mostly animal furs (primarily the beaver), which were of immense value to the fashion and hat-making industries of Europe. However, as fashions changed and as the beaver were hunted to near extinction in this area, the beaver pelts became less important and the trade shifted to other commodities. Over the years, the North American trade became less oriented toward receiving the furs and more toward selling the manufactured goods to the native Americans.

The fort, and the trading community which grew up around it were located at the water's edge (as described by later visitors) where the canoes of the voyageurs could be unloaded with ease. Though overlooked by the bluffs from both sides of the river, the site was considered secure since the nearby villages of local Indians were firmly allied to the French. This is particularly true of the Potawatomi, who migrated into the area and became the dominant tribe soon after the fort was constructed. They were considered by the French to be among the most dependable of their Indian allies.

A rather fanciful 17th century European artist's interpretation of beaver hunting.

The community which grew up around the fort was based on the trade with the Potawatomi and other area Indians. Its economic sphere of influence reached out for several hundred miles and controlled and guarded the vital St. Joseph/Kankakee River portage. This portage was the most reliable (in terms of water and weather conditions) and the most convenient of several that connected the Great Lakes with the Mississippi River. This was the main communications link between the French colonies in Canada and those in the lower Mississippi and Gulf Coast regions. For the most part, trade and communications were restricted to the times of the year when the rivers were not frozen over.

The canoe was the vehicle which was used in this trade. This type of boat was developed by the native Americans long before the Europeans arrived and used in their own pre-historic commerce. With the growth of the fur trade the building and use of the canoe expanded greatly into almost an industry. In the regions to the north where the birch trees grew big enough to provide the large sheets of bark needed to make canoes, whole villages turned into canoe building factories. They built and traded their canoes for other necessities. The large freight canoes used on the greater waterways were as much as 45 feet long, capable of hauling four or five tons of cargo and requiring a minimum crew of six paddlers. At times, crews as large as 16 were used for special purposes.

The men who paddled the canoes were known as *voyageurs*. They were usually young men who were attracted to the freedom and adventure of the fur trade. Paddling the canoes was the "entry level" job in the trade and many if not most of the successful traders started out at the canoe level. The work was hard and the living conditions were harsh, but there never seems to have been a shortage of voyageurs to paddle upstream.

Voyageurs did not usually risk valuable cargos by shooting rapids but passengers could be given a thrilling ride.

Canoes provided all of the transportation in the Great Lakes and connecting rivers for over 100 years. Fleets of canoes would set out from Montreal in the spring as soon as the ice melted on the rivers, destined for the various fur trading posts scattered across the French territories.

After weeks of paddling, the voyageurs and their canoes would arrive at posts like Fort Saint Joseph. Their arrival was a time of celebration for the residents since it meant the arrival of news, new goods for trade and for their own consumption, old friends and new faces as well.

It also was the time to send back to the East the quantities of furs, hides, corn, maple sugar, etc., that they had accumulated in trade over the winter and early spring. While other voyageur canoes made trips at other times when the river conditions allowed, by far the largest share of the trade occurred in these annual fleets. After spending all too brief a time at the outposts, the canoes would be loaded with the accumulation of furs and other cargo. The passengers returning to the East would board, and the arduous return trip would begin.

Life at an outpost like Fort Saint Joseph was geared to the cycles of the weather. Spring thaw, and winter ice-up, controlled the timing of the voyageur flotillas. The weather also controlled the lifestyle pattern of the Potawatomi, upon whom the traders and their families depended for their livelihood. The Potawatomi followed a cycle of seasonal village or camping locations. As spring started to arrive, they moved from their winter village sites to maple groves where they would camp, while they produced quantities of maple sugar for their own use and to trade to the French. As spring progressed they would relocate to the areas where they could plant their garden fields of corn, beans, and squash. They also exploited the annual spring runs of the fish in the rivers and streams. As summer progressed, they moved a little further north into the summer hunting areas where ripening wild fruit was also available. As fall arrived, they would return to their garden campsites to harvest and process their crops. With the onset of winter they traveled to their wintering villages. These winter villages were in locations which provided shelter, ade-

The arrival of the voyageurs was eagerly awaited especially when — as in this case — they brought the men's wives as well as the supplies. This is the arrival in 1701 of the voyageurs at Detroit which had been founded earlier that year.

11

quate fuel, and where they could trap and hunt for animals whose thick winter pelts were the most valuable in trade and most useful for making warm winter clothing. The residents of the Fort Saint Joseph community were thoroughly immersed in the Potawatomi cycle. Everyone, soldier, civilian and priest, depended on them for much of their existence. Much of the food they ate was purchased from the Potawatomi. A portion of the French community was indeed part native itself. For generations, traders had married into the Indian clans and much of French Canada was genetically as well as culturally of mixed-blood or *Metis* descent.

The residents' trade with the Indians was their basic reason for being here. Over the years the Potawatomi had become dependent on the traders for the manufactured goods which they needed to survive (having long since given up their stone-age toolmaking techniques). A mutually dependent relationship had developed which biologists would call "symbiotic" (a community made up of two components which require each other in order to survive). This cooperation resulted in nearly a century of harmony between the local Indians and the French residents. It also assisted with the transition when the British took over the area later on, and made the adjustment to the arrival of the Anglo-American settlers less difficult.

During its early phases the Fort community was dominated by the military, although the French system of interrelated business, military, and religious interests make clear distinctions difficult. Promoting the commerce of the fur trade and the missions was in the best interest of the military since it helped secure the peaceful allegiance of the Indians. At the same time, the trade helped finance and supply the military garrisons and missionaries. At times, in fact, the French system actually "franchised" the trade to the military officers who would bid for the privilege of operating a post. An officer would pay the government for the privilege of commanding a post. He was then expected to pay not only his own salary, but that of all of his men, as well as the operating costs of the post out of his profits from the trade. This early "military/industrial complex" signalled all kinds of potential problems so it was later replaced. In the early years, however, the commanding officer played a paternalistic role in the community, even to the extent of performing baptisms and marriages in the absence of the priest. One of the effects of this system was that a family often came to control a community over several generations as the command of the post was passed from father to son in an almost feudal manner. The Fort Saint Joseph community was not exempt from this. From the 1720's to the 1740's it was basically controlled by the members of the de Villiers family, from father to son, and on to son-in-law. Members of this family were to have a significant impact on the course of history for all of North America.

From its establishment in 1691 until the British takeover in the early 1760's the fort and community basically enjoyed a peaceful existence. At times military events in other parts of the country required the presence of its regular soldiers (or *Troupes de la Marine*) as well as the militia (made up of all of the able-bodied men between the ages of fifteen or sixteen and sixty) from the community.

Men from Fort Saint Joseph, both Canadian and Indian were present and involved in many of the famous engagements of the years of war between the French and the British in North America.

An officer of the Troupes de la Marine of the Languedoc Regiment

12

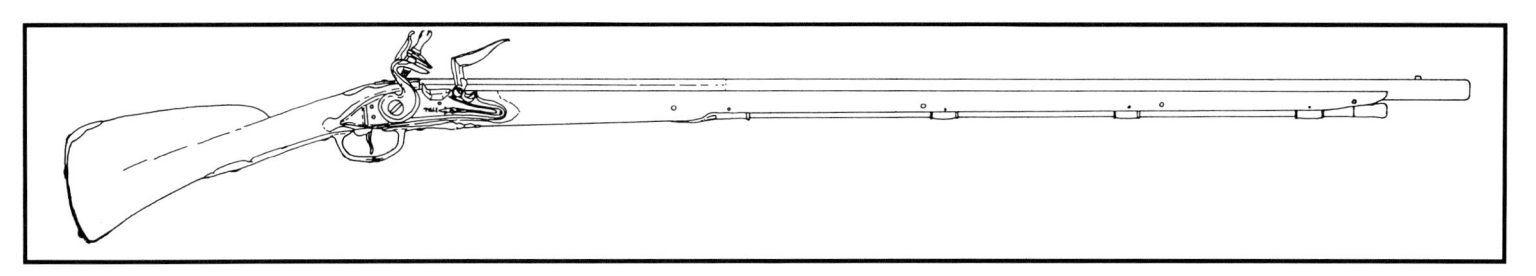

Flintlock firearms of this type — a smooth bore musket — were used by Indians and French alike to gather food and animal skins. Their use as a weapon was secondary for civilians.

French soldiers spent most of their time at Fort Saint Joseph engaged in agricultural or construction work, or helping with the fur trade to supplement their meager pay.

During most of this era, Fort St. Joseph played an important role in securing the friendly relations with the Potawatomi and other area Indians by supplying their needs for blankets, pots and pans, tools, firearms and ammunition, and all of the hundreds of other manufactured items, on which they had come to depend. It was also important in recruiting the young Indian warriors for operations in other areas. However, in the 1720's, during one phase of the war against the Fox, (a tribe of war-like and violently anti-French Indians who lived in what is now western Illinois), the Fort was the gathering place of several thousand soldiers and Indian warriors from all over French North America. They met there to launch the summer's campaign against the Fox tribe and their allies.

With the exception of the various military campaigns which required the services of some of the men from the post, life at Fort Saint Joseph peacefully followed the seasonal and trading cycles. The governmental methods for controlling the trade with the Indians (which was considered a tool of foreign policy) were changed several times over the years. The systems usually consisted of licenses or permits issued for each canoe-load and crew. The permits or licenses regulated the type and amount of goods which would be allowed to be traded to the Indians and specified the destination of the canoe load. As this system was developed, the trade came to be dominated by civilian traders.

Beginning in the 1740's a trader named Louis Chevallier started to operate at Fort Saint Joseph. He was a member of a large family from Fort Michillimakinac. His father was involved in the trade as were his numerous brothers and brothers-in-law. Such kinship ties linked almost all of the major traders. Louis Chevallier gradually came to dominate the trade at Fort Saint Joseph and in later years actually owned almost the entire community. Under his leadership, the post reached its peak numbering nearly 200 residents.

At Fort Saint Joseph, as elsewhere, the trade was carried out on a basis of credit and barter. There was little cash money in circulation. The Indians obtained needed supplies for the winter on the promise to pay in the spring with their yet to be trapped winter pelts. Accumulated furs were shipped back to Montreal where their value was credited to the traders' account with the Montreal merchants. These merchants, in turn, shipped furs to and received goods back from Europe on credit. The trader would draw on his credit with the Montreal merchants to order his supply of goods to trade with the Indians, and to supply his own needs and those of the other Europeans at his post. The fur trade was a risky but profitable business. It attracted an independent and courageous type of individual. The changing fashions in Europe affected the fur values. Isolation at the end of a long and fragile supply and communication chain, shifting government policy, bad hunting conditions, unstable Indian relations, or an overturned canoe, all could spell ruin. Because of these conditions, being a trader and having one's lifetime assets tied up in the trade involved a long-term commitment to the business.

In the late 1740's and early 1750's, French and British interests in North America came into conflict again. The Anglo-American colonists, who were initially settled along the seaboard, were reaching farther and farther into the interior, passing through the eastern mountian barrier and into the Ohio River valley, which had long been considered French territory. The initial incidents involved conflicts between English traders who encroached upon the French trade along the present day Ohio-Pennsylvania border. Over the years this conflict slowly escalated until the French-Canadian government decided to establish a chain of military posts from the shores of eastern Lake Erie to the headwaters of the Ohio River, at the site of present day Pittsburgh, to protect their trade. As in most of the Colonial wars in North America, this conflict was only part of a greater world-wide war between France and England. The conflict over the trade was exacerbated by the claims of the wealthy Anglo-American land speculators who had formed the Ohio Company. They claimed title to huge tracts of land in the area west of the mountains in French territory.

In order to profit from these tracts, the speculators (who were often allied with colonial government officials) had first to evict the French from their outposts. They would then drive out or otherwise pacify the resident Indians and sell the land to settlers. The officials of the Ohio Company persuaded the governor of Virginia to send a message to the French outposts demanding that they vacate the land that the Ohio Company claimed. The French, of course, refused to leave their own territory. The representative that the governor sent was a young, 21-year-old Virginia militia officer, Major George Washington.

"a native woodland hunter" by Fred Threlfall
used with permission

....I met in ye woods an Indian who tells me that he formerly was given a brown coat, blew cotton shirt, a hat and hunting gun by ye commander of ye French fort in return for supplying meat for the garrison there......"

George Washington as portrayed in an early Currier & Ives print.

The governor of Virgina and the Ohio Company were intent on enforcing their demands, and sent a small party of soldiers into the area to build a British fort to validate and enforce their claims. Washington was sent back with another detachment in May of 1754 to reinforce the fort building party — which, unknown to him, had already been forced out by the French. The French, in turn, sent out a party with a diplomatic messenger demanding that Washington's group of English intruders withdraw. This French envoy was another young officer, Ensign Joseph Coulon de Villiers, Sieur de Jumonville, formerly of Fort Saint Joseph. He was one of the members of the family of de Villiers who had been in command at Fort Saint Joseph for so many years.

The two parties tragically crossed paths in the wilderness of western Pennsylvania. Washington's party was able to confront the French group by surprising them at dawn in their camp. It is possible that it was accidental — a matter of quite some historical debate — but shots were fired before communications could be established. After a brief exchange of shots, the French envoy and his party were all killed or captured. One of the few survivors escaped and was able to make his way back to the French at Fort Duquesne (Pittsburgh) and report the deaths of Jumonville and the rest of the delegation.

Washington, realizing that he had stirred up a hornet's nest, retreated a few miles to a slightly more defensible position. There he built a small field fortification in expectation of French retaliation and hopes of reinforcements. The expected French response was not long in coming. The death of Jumonville, and his party occurred on the 28th of May. Shortly thereafter, Louis Coulon de Villiers, Jumonville's older brother who had been in command at Fort St. Joseph from 1742 to 1745, arrived at Fort Duquesne. He requested and obtained command of the combined French and Indian forces which were getting ready to attack Washington. Washington and his men were still at the little fort they had named Fort Necessity.

The attack commenced on the 3rd of July. The battle took only one day. With the tiny fort surrounded, casualties rising, and no hope of reinforcements, Washington quickly, and probably with great relief, surrendered. The surrender terms were magnanimous. The Virginian party was allowed to leave with their wounded and their weapons and with full military honor. They would even be allowed to come back later to get the baggage and equipment they could not carry off with them. However, the surrender documents (written in French) which Washington signed contained the admission that he had "assassinated" Jumonville. He, of course, later claimed that his translator had mistranslated the surrender documents. The French made great political use of this admission when the documents finally reached Montreal, Quebec, and Paris.

An artist's interpretation of Fort Necessity based on the most recent archaeological research. The wounded and the supplies were put inside the circular palisade and the cabin. The defending soldiers took shelter and fired from behind the dirt embankment.

> *The Jumonville Affair, as it is called, is considered to be the start of the Seven Years War in North America. American historians have called it the French and Indian War. The ironic thing about this incident is that it nearly had a disastrous effect in later years. During the American Revolution, when Ben Franklin and the other American diplomats were desperately seeking French assistance against the British, George Washington's undiplomatic act of "assassinating" an official French envoy on a diplomatic mission was used by anti-American factions as an argument against French support. Some of the French court officials also tried to use it to make the replacement of Washington as commander of the American forces with a French general a condition of French support. Fortunately for the course of events other opinions prevailed.*

The Seven Years (or French and Indian) War brought to an end the rule of France over Fort Saint Joseph. With the victory of General Wolfe over the French army outside Quebec, and the subsequent surrender of the French-Canadian government at Montreal, all of the little French communities in the heartland of the continent were isolated. Though their forces had won most of the frontier battles, the war was lost in other parts of the world. To the victors went the spoils — all of Canada. It took the British some time to consolidate their new dominion. The French surrendered in 1760. Almost a year later the first British soldiers arrived to raise the Union Jack over the trading community of Fort Saint Joseph. During this time, the remaining French-Canadian military and those civilians who could afford to do so left. Some may have gone back to France, while many emigrated south and west to the area around present-day St. Louis, Missouri. The French territories there had been ceded to Spain, but the former French communities there still remained French in custom and language, with only a very thin veneer of Spanish officialdom in the top governmental positions.

Because of their long-term investment in the trade, their lines of commerce linked through now British Montreal, and the inability to liquidate their assets, some of the population of Fort Saint Joseph stayed behind when their friends, relatives and neighbors left. Among the remaining group was Louis Chevallier. As the leading man in the community, he had been entrusted with the custody of the French Governmental property by the departing French commander with instructions to turn them over when the British arrived.

Fort Saint Joseph was occupied by a small detachment of the 60th Royal American Regiment in October of 1760. This regiment was recruited in the colonies for the regular British army rather than a colonial militia unit. This small group, no more than a dozen and a half men, were commanded by Ensign Francis Schlosser. He was young, immature, and even for that era, overly fond of alcohol. He also had a very strong prejudice (common among the British) against their new French and Indian subjects. His prejudice, incompetency, poor judgement, and immoderate behavior would cost his men dearly.

Soldiers of the 60th Royal American Regiment were massacred at Fort Saint Joseph in Pontiac's uprising.

As the British took over the Great Lakes area, they attempted to reduce the tremendous expense that the French had incurred in securing their relations with the Indians. In spite of warnings from the officers who were in contact with the Indians, the British headquarters in Quebec, as a cost cutting measure, ordered that the "giving of presents" and supplying of arms and ammunition be discontinued. The giving of presents was a part of the complex but necessary process whereby the French had long maintained their Indian allies. The provision of arms, ammunition and other supplies on credit or as outright gifts was vitally necessary to help the Indians get through the winter. This sudden change of policy was a terrible blow to the Indians. A large number of them, from many different tribes, had gathered at Detroit. Meeting together in a unity seldom found among them, they attempted to put forward an organized repeal of the new policy. Their nominal leader, Pontiac, met with the British commander, but to no avail. British policy was fixed, and the Indians began to consider desperate measures. This unfortunate circumstance was apparently manipulated by some of the Detroit area French who misled the Indians into the belief that if the Indians would strike against the British, the French too would rise up and join them in throwing out the British conquerors. The Indians formed what has become known as "Pontiac's conspiracy," in which the Indians would strike concerted blows against all of the isolated British garrisons in the former French territory. In this bloody uprising, all but two of the British garrisons fell to the Indians. Fort Pitt, the former French Fort Dusquene, held out with difficulty — and early biological warfare. The commander saw to it that the clothing and blankets of the victims of a smallpox outbreak within the fort fell into the hands of the besieging Indians — with devastating effect. Ravaged by the disease for which they had no natural immunity, they were forced to lift the siege. Detroit was the other post that held out. Warned by someone who had access to the Indian councils (probably a French resident), the British were able to thwart the planned surprise attack and withstand the ensuing siege by using the Detroit River to reinforce and resupply the fort there.

Fort Michillimakinac was taken when the Indians turned a game of "baggitaway" (lacrosse) into a massacre by pursuing their ball into the fort and then drawing hidden weapons.

At Fort Saint Joseph a different story was to be told. By alienating both the local Indians and the local French with his behavior, Schlosser had doomed most of his men. When emissaries from Pontiac's gathering arrived to persuade the local Potawatomi to join the conspiracy, Louis Chevallier was able to persuade most of the local Potawatomi to stay out of the affair. Eventually, only a few of the younger warriors and the visitors from the Detroit group agreed to attack the British. Chevallier attempted to warn the British to be on their guard, but his warning was arrogantly and rudely rejected. The next day, by a ruse, armed Indians gained access to the normally secured British quarters where they quickly overwhelmed the unarmed and un-alerted soldiers. All but two or three were killed and the survivors, including Schlosser, were taken captive. They were later exchanged for an Indian leader the British had captured. Upon his release, Schlosser had the audacity to demand that the British government reimburse him for the loss of his personal property in the attack. Ultimately, Pontiac's Conspiracy failed, but it did cause delays in the British consolidation of their newly acquired territories. Fort Saint Joseph itself was never again assigned a permanent military garrison, though it was occupied at times by visiting detachments of troops. It remained a vital link in the British control of the Great Lakes Region. The British retained control by appointing Louis Chevallier to a position as the "King's man;" a semi-official position representing the British government to the Indians with whom he had developed a great deal of influence. He was appointed by the commander of the British forces at Michillimakinac who was the top authority for the western Great Lakes area. Fort Saint Joseph was considered a dependent post of Michillimakinac and Chevallier reported to the commanding officer there. During the years between the end of Pontiac's uprising and the beginnings of the American War of Independence affairs progressed peacefully and successfully. With the expanding garrisons at Michillimakinac and the growing town of Detroit, the market for Indian-grown food supplies increased to the point that the large canoes were no longer adequate for bulk cargos. In order to profit from the business of supplying agricultural commodities, John

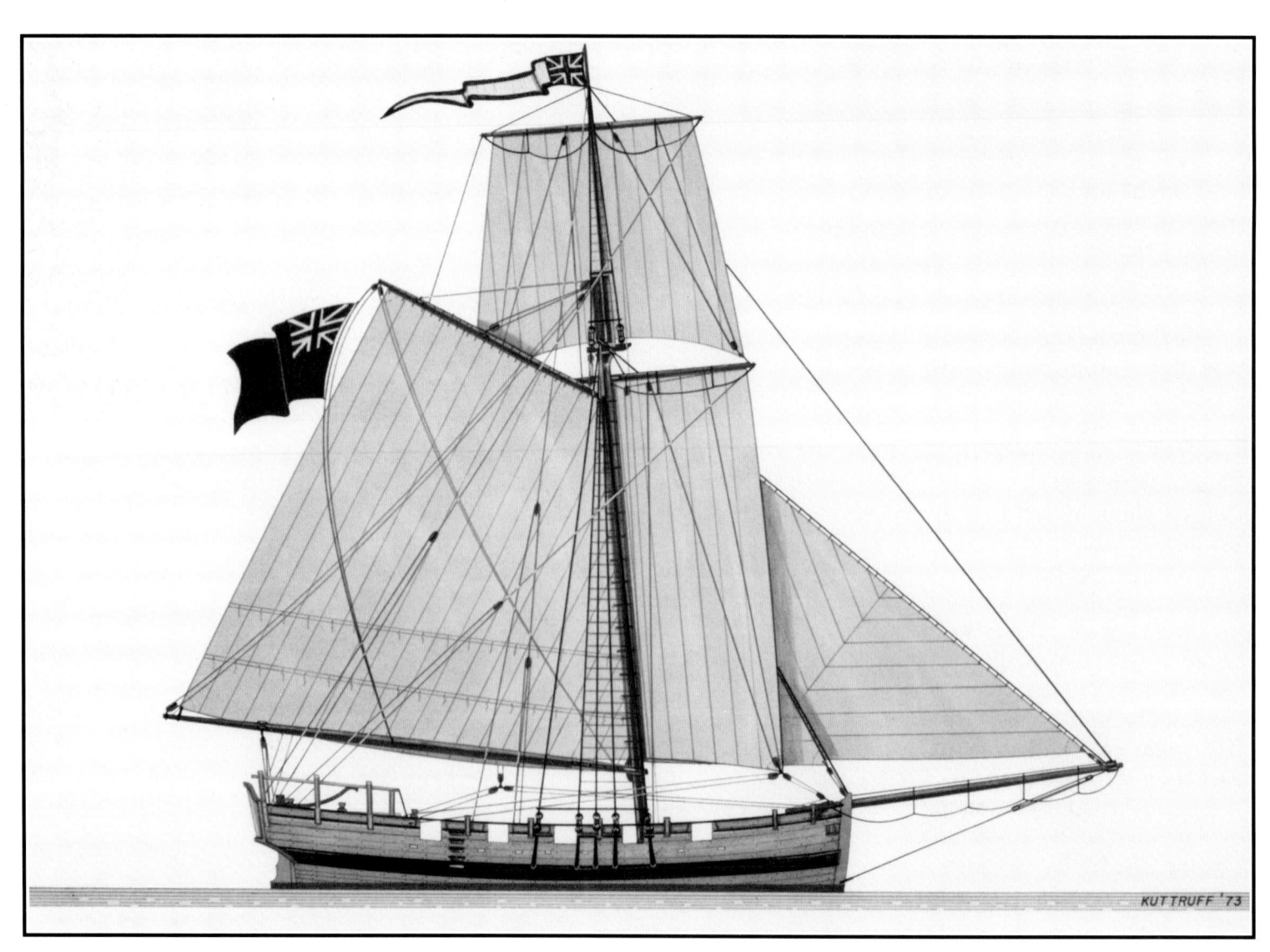

The *Welcome* was the first successful sailing vessel on the Great Lakes.
It was built to ship bulky cargo more efficiently than the voyageur.

Askins, a trading partner and friend of Louis Chevallier, built in 1775 the first sailing ship on the Great Lakes since La Salle's long-lost *Griffin*. His ship, the *Welcome* was built to travel around the lakes visiting the mouths of the various rivers to meet the Indian canoes laden with corn and other produce.

As the 1770's progressed, the political situation began to change as resentment of British policy began to grow in the colonies. This resentment turned into rebellion along the eastern seaboard and on July 4, 1776, the former British colonies declared themselves independent. At first this revolutionary event had little impact on the community of Fort Saint Joseph. But as the war progressed the situation began to change. Most of the conventional military activity of the War of Independence took place in the East. A different form of war took place in the heartland of the continent where British, French, Spanish, and now American interests came into conflict.

Other than the fact that the exchange of their supplies came via the St. Lawrence River and the lakes, the British and their French subjects in the Great Lakes area had little to do with events of the war during its early years. However, the British naval blockade of the eastern ports caused the Continental Congress and some of the state governments to look to the Mississippi River as a possible "back door" for necessary arms and ammunition. If such supplies could be brought up the Mississippi and Ohio Rivers they could then be moved overland to supply the eastern armies, thus thwarting the blockade. George Rogers Clark and a detachment of the Virginia state forces were sent to secure the passage of these goods by establishing a military base in the lower Ohio and central Mississippi valley. His activities in this area, greatly assisted by the longtime French residents, and the under-the-table help of the Spanish Colonial administration presented the heretofore complacent British with a major crisis. They attempted to ruin Clark's plans by sending an expeditionary force from Detroit to Vincennes. The British force was defeated by the near-legendary march that Clark, his Virginia troops, and the pro-American French militia companies made across the frozen and flooded Illinois country to surprise and capture Governor Hamilton at Fort Sackville in Vincennes.

Another reason for Clark's activities was to strike back against the British and pro-British French who had been leading numerous Indian war parties against American frontier settlements. Part of Clark's strategy for forestalling these raids was to launch attacks against the British western posts and against Detroit where Governor Hamilton had initiated and sponsored the policy of using the Indians.

With the much-hated "Hair-buyer Hamilton" (the Americans called him that because he was reputed to

The surrender of Fort Sackville at present-day Vincennes had a tremendous impact on the military and political course of events in the Great Lakes region.

have put a cash bounty on settlers' scalps) in captivity after the capture of Fort Sackville, the British forces in the Great Lakes were stripped of their leader. This caused a reshuffling of British commanders in the Great Lakes area which in turn caused great problems for the community at Fort Saint Joseph (or the St. Joseph's Post as it was often called by the British during this era).

The Commander at Fort Michillimakinac, DePeyster, who had a long and congenial relationship with the French from St. Joseph's Post, was transferred to Detroit to replace now-prisoner Hamilton as military commander. A new lieutenant governor was installed in his place at the Straits. Though he had than military) a year or more previously, Patrick Sinclair had been delayed from assuming his post because of the war. Not only was Sinclair the leading civil authority he was also the ranking officer in the British military at Michillimakinac. He had purchased rank, a normal British practice at that time, in order to command the military as well as the civilians.

Unlike Depeyster, Sinclair took an early and powerful dislike to the Frenchmen at Fort Saint Joseph. In addition to the more or less normal anti-French prejudices common to the British, Sinclair seems to have had additional negative feelings. These were exacerbated by the fact that in 1778 the French nation had joined the conflict by declaring war on Great Britain, followed the next year by a similar declaration by Spain. George Rogers Clark now had official support of the Spanish Government as well as the support of the French population in his efforts against the British.

The people of Fort Saint Joseph aggravated him further by refusing to trade by the rules the British had set up. All of the trade from Fort Saint Joseph was supposed to go through Michillimakinac. However, since the days of the French and Indian War, the Potawatomi of the St. Joseph River area had been using horses (traditionally acquired at Gen. Braddock's defeat). It was far easier for them to take their trade across country, via the Great Sauk Trail, to Detroit where supplies were greater, prices were cheaper and their old friend DePeyster was in command. The Potawatomi people were not considered to be canoe-oriented Indians. Furthermore they lived far south of areas where canoe-quality birch could be found. Canoes for traveling to Michillimakinac had to be purchased and voyageurs hired, and the prices had increased greatly. It made much more sense to them to go to Detroit. It did not make sense, however, to Sinclair, who carried on a long and angry correspondence with the parties concerned. He was convinced that his authority was undermined and that the traders at Michillimakinac were being hurt. While it was the Potawatomi who were doing this, Sinclair laid the blame on the French — particularly on Louis Chevallier.

Louis Chevallier was attempting to walk a political and economic tightrope. He was a Frenchman who had become an English subject. All of his financial interests, no matter what his personal opinions, had to be in the British cause since they controlled his supply line. (However not all of the French living in English territory were loyal to the British, even prior to the French declaration of war.) Chevallier had been appointed "King's man" by DePeyster and established as an Indian agent. It was his responsibility, in Sinclair's view, to keep the Indians firmly in line with the British efforts.

Fort Saint Joseph was supposed to be an early warning station, gathering intelligence of Clark's activities to the south and passing reliable information back to Michillimakinac. Sinclair became convinced that Chevallier and the rest of the French at Fort Saint Joseph were secretly siding with the Patriot cause. It is hard to determine exactly why he would feel this way. Perhaps other traders who wished to take over the St. Joseph's trade influenced him. Perhaps the neutral attitude that the Indians attempted to maintain (accepting presents and blandishments from both sides but taking no action in support of either) in spite of Chevallier's efforts fueled his suspicions. Maybe it was a long antipathy of the French in general. Maybe the man was paranoid — he seems to have shown a streak of mental instability. Perhaps it was a combination — or possibly he was right and Chevallier was playing a double game. If so the evidence is long lost which would prove the case.

In the summer of 1779 things had come to a head. Rumors were flying that the long dreaded offensive of Clark's combined Patriot and French forces was about to be launched. Chevallier dutifully sent in the reports of the rumors. Consequently, a strong detachment made up of British soldiers, pro-British French militia, armed voyageurs and Indian allies amounting to nearly 200 men including members of the King's 8th Regiment arrived at the Saint Joseph's Post to wait in ambush for the Patriot army. By this time, the old French fortifications were long gone, so this expeditionary force camped outside the village. They soon found out that they were the victim of a grand military hoax. Clark was not on the march. He could not get the supplies he needed. Then to add insult to British embarrassment a grand Indian conference called by the expedition's leader, Lieutenant Thomas

Though Lt. Col. George Rogers Clark never set foot in the Saint Joseph River valley, his activities in the French/Spanish settlements to the south had a tremendous effect on the course of events at the Saint Joseph settlement. This portrait was made later in his life.

Bennett of the King's 8th Regiment, was a total fiasco. Not only did the Indians, mostly Potawatomi, refuse to enlist in the British cause, they had heard that France had entered the war and they announced that they would follow the lead of their old traditional ally, the French. On top of that, Bennett's men just missed meeting their resupply vessel and had to make an ignominious, hungry, and uncomfortable retreat back to Michillimakinac.

Their only accomplishment of note was the capture and arrest of Jean Baptiste Pointe du Sable, a French-mulatto trader, who was suspected of being a Patriot agent. He had been trading at the mouth of Trail Creek in present-day Michigan City, Indiana. After being confined at Fort Saint Joseph, he was taken back to Michillimakinac as a prisoner, only to be released because of a lack of evidence. Du Sable later returned to the area, eventually settling at the mouth of the Chicago River. He is considered by some to be the "founder" of the City of Chicago.

For whatever his motives, Sinclair determined to do away with the French problem here. In the spring of 1780, he sent a small fleet of canoes commanded by one of Chevallier's nephews, Louis Joseph Ainsee, to evacuate the post. After a quick census of those present (he counted 48 residents) Ainsee loaded almost all the residents into the canoes and returned them to Michillimakinac as prisoners. From there they were dispersed without trial back to Canada. Louis Chevallier protested his unfair treatment to no apparent avail.

While some traders of proven loyalty were sent back to provide for the Indian's needs, they were not liked by the Potawatomi who petitioned to have their old friends and relations returned. Such petitions were fruitless. Sinclair felt that it was the consequence of their lack of loyalty and justly deserved. The only French left were those who had escaped into the woods or were away at the time of the arrests. Word of the treatment of the St. Joseph's French spread among the other French scattered among the small trading communities of the Great Lake, Ohio, and Illinois countries. It certainly did little to endear them to the British side, and it set the stage for the final events in the history of Fort Saint Joseph.

The British continued to send shipments of militarily useful supplies to the new traders at Fort Saint Joseph. A loyalist French Lieutenant in the Indian Service (though civilians, Indian Service men were given military rank) by the name of Dagneau De Quindre was placed in charge of the fort. By this time the old palisades were long gone and the fort undoubtedly consisted of a number of warehouses, trading shops, civilian residences, and various agricultural structures. Soon the warehouses were full of the material for war because the British hoped to sponsor a massive Indian raid on the pro-American settlements around the St. Louis area. These settlements, Cahokia, St. Genevieve, Praire du Rocher, and St. Louis itself, were the area where many of the St. Joseph's French had resettled when they fled from the British back in 1760. Among them were close relatives and friends of Louis Chevallier.

At about this same time a military officer from France by the name of LaBalme arrived in the St. Louis area. He was trying to create fame, and probably fortune, for himself by organizing the French of the area into an army. By playing upon the cultural differences between them and Clark's Virginians he was able to promote an independent military operation which was intended to do away with the British threat to the north. LaBalme developed a grandiose scheme for several different simultaneous attacks against Detroit and Fort Saint Joseph. He expected the local French to rise up and help him overthrow the British. Unfortunately for LaBalme, his plans were ruined when his small force, which was headed for Detroit, stopped at the British trading posts (at present day Fort Wayne, Indiana) and proceeded to loot them. The local Indians there, who were pro-British, took offense at the pillaging and attacked LaBalme's little army (probably less than 100 men). LaBalme was killed, as were many of his men. The rest retreated quickly back to the St. Louis settlements.

LaBalme's proposed attack on the warehouses of Fort Saint Joseph resulted in little more success. A small group commanded by Jean Baptiste Hamelin

---

Louis Chevallier's petition after his arrest. It was addressed to the General Haldimand, the British Commander of North America.

"May it please your Excellency.......
The very humble address of Louis Chevallier, formerly a merchant at St. Joseph's successively employed for a number of years by the Commandants of Michillimakinac to maintain the Indians in their duty toward his Majesty.......for about thirty five years. That on the 25th of that same month...Mr. Ainsee having orders from Mr. Sinclair....voluntarily or by force, to bring all the inhabitants of the Post (St. Joseph's) to Michillimakinac. Your petitioner began to obey.....sixty-eight years of age, his wife of seventy, having all of his fortune in the neighborhood, ten houses, good lands, orchards, gardens, cattle, furniture, utensils, and debts, all of which he has made an entire sacrifice to obedience.........He humbly hopes to ask...that he be permitted to return to St. Joseph's to gather together the remains of his fortune....."

His petition was ignored, and he died in poverty a few years later.

made its way from Cahokia on horseback to the fort. Upon arrival there in early December of 1780, they found the place undefended and almost unoccupied. Lieutenant DeQuindre and the rest of the Indians and traders had gone off on the winter hunt in the swamps of the Kankakee. Hamelin's raiding party of 16 men was able to loot whatever goods had value enough to make it worth the effort to haul them back without facing any resistance. They then attempted to beat a hasty retreat. DeQuindre and the hunting party had been informed of the raid and immediately set out after the raiders. They found the Cahokians camped in the sand dunes at the south end of Lake Michigan and quickly overwhelmed them. (A historical marker in Indiana Dunes State Park near Chesterton, Indiana, marks the supposed site of the "Battle of the Dunes.") Of the 16 raiders only five escaped the rest were killed or wounded and captured. Contrary to some of the "legends of the lost treasure of old Fort Saint Joseph," all of the trade goods stolen (there were no bags of silver or gold coins at the fort) were returned to the warehouses at the fort. The surviving captives were sent to Detroit for possible hanging as spies.

At almost the same time that this incident was taking place, a different group of St. Louis area French and a group of anti-British Potawatomi Indians were developing a plan that would spell the end for the fort.

Eugene Pourré was the commander of the 2nd Company of the St. Louis Militia, one of the armed and drilled citizen-soldier groups common to almost all French-Canadian communities. The local militia groups had been active the previous year in repelling a British sponsored Indian attack on the St. Louis area settlements.

These former French militia companies were under the overall command of the Spanish governmental authorities so they could be considered Spanish militia even though they were made up of French Canadians.

Two of the Potawatomi leaders who had become very anti-British, Naquigen and *El Heturno* (French: *Le Tourneau* — The Blackbird), visited St. Louis in late 1780 and demanded through an interpreter that the Spanish authorities (according to the Spanish records) allow them to attack Fort Saint Joseph. The Spanish Lieutenant-Governor in charge of the area, Francisco Cruzat, not only gave the Indians permission, he also authorized Captain Pourré to assemble and lead a volunteer party of the French militia in the attack. The fact that this attack was made under the auspices of the Spanish and the fact that it was first reported via the Spanish newspapers has led to the expedition being called "the Spanish Raid" even though the raiding party was made up of Indians and French volunteers.

The Spanish feared the loss of influence among the Indians if they did not allow the attack. In addition, they probably wished to see the military supplies being stockpiled at the fort destroyed before they could be used. The French militia detachment may have wished to get revenge for the defeat of the LaBalme/Hamelin group a month previously. All parties concerned may have also hoped to gain from seizing the stockpiled supplies. This would have been possible since the supplies needed to motivate and equip a large scale Indian raiding party would have included quantities of regular trade goods, clothing, pots and pans, blankets, brandy and rum, as well as weapons and ammunition. All of these items would have been "fair game" to the raiders.

The members of the raiding party consisted of about 65 militia, Pourré in charge, and an equal number of Indians who left the St. Louis area on January 2, 1781. After a long and difficult journey, they arrived at the local Potawatomi Indian winter villages where they persuaded the Indians to remain neutral — for a share of the loot.

During the pre-dawn hours of February 12 they crossed the frozen river on the ice (it had been an unusually cold winter) and surprised the resident traders in their beds. Upon capturing the traders without firing a shot, they raised a Spanish flag provided by Lt. Gov. Cruzat and read a proclamation claiming the territory in the name of Spain. They then proceeded to loot, pillage, and burn the stockpiles. Goods that were too bulky or not valuable

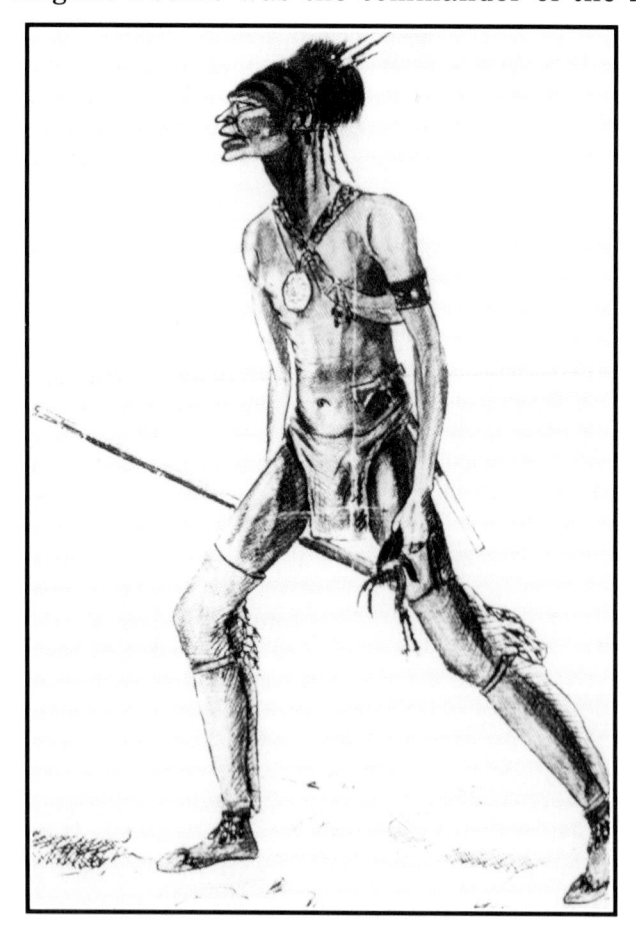

In the 1750's George Townshend made this sketch of a Great Lakes area Indian warrior returning from a successful encounter.

enough to justify the effort to carry back were broken, burned, or otherwise rendered useless. Any of the surviving buildings that were of military significance were also razed. Pourré was well aware of the fate of Hamelin's raiding party. After only one day he had his men back on the trail to St. Louis.

It was well he did, for Lt. DeQuindre arrived and attempted to rally the Potawatomi as he had done earlier to follow and ambush the raiders. However, the Potawatomi refused — perhaps overawed by the size of the group.

Though the St. Joseph's Potawatomi asked the British to send more traders to them, their requests were denied. It was felt that they were too unreliable and that they should be punished for their failure to resist the Spanish Raid.

With the end of the American Revolution, affairs in the Great Lakes area were left in a state of confusion. The new United States placed greater emphasis on the requirements for governing the states along the East Coast and, more or less, ignored the heartland areas. The British refused to withdraw their troops from the interior because of a failure of the U.S. Government to satisfy British claims for damages. The local Indians, however, were able to get their needed supplies from several traders who established stores in the area. A French Canadian by the name of LeClare or LeClerc (early records are inconsistent in their spelling) took over the trade at the former fort location. According to Indian tradition, he utilized the few surviving structures for his business. LeClerc was also a blacksmith who provided vital blacksmithing and gunsmithing services to the Indians. In addition, William Burnette operated a trading post on the river a mile or two upstream from the river's mouth at Lake Michigan.

About this time the Indians relocated their winter villages (as they did periodically) to the place where the southern branch of the Old Sauk Trail forded the river, a few miles to the south of the location of the old French community. LeClerc also relocated his trading and blacksmithing post to be closer to his customers. Local legend is that in the process he (or Joseph Bertrand who succeeded him as trader shortly thereafter) also moved the chapel of the Jesuit mission for use as part of his trading store. The new location was known as *parc aux vaches,* apparently because in previous years it had been an area where the eastern woods bison had been found. In later years it came to be known as Bertrand (named after the trader-turned-land developer who platted it).

The years between the end of the Revolutionary War and the arrival of the Anglo-American settlers in the 1820's and '30's were difficult years. There was an ongoing frontier war between many of the Indian tribes and the Americans who were starting to move into Ohio and southern Indiana. This was encouraged and directed by the British, who had still not vacated the area. Yet at the same time traders like Burnette, LeClerc, Bertrand and others continued to supply the Indian's needs. The U.S. government also supplied the Indians by making annual payments of goods (annuity payments) to the tribes in exchange for the title to vast areas of their ancestral territories. The British also made "presents" to the Indian tribes who journeyed to Canada regularly. The era of the fur trade in the Great Lakes was over. The beaver were long gone, and the Indians had little else but their land to exchange for the manufactured goods they now had become dependent on. Even their dealings with the traders were now often based, not on credit for anticipated furs and agricultural products, but on the anticipated spring or fall annuity payments. As treaty after treaty was signed, the Indian lands were gradually bought by the government and the land opened up for the arrival of Anglo-American settlers from the east.

Niles' native Norman DeLay carefully researched this sketch to illustrate the raising of the Spanish flag over Fort Saint Joseph on February 12, 1781 by the French Militia from St. Louis.

Monuments and Markers

The 1876 Centennial of the Nation stimulated a tremendous interest in the nation's past. That interest was accelerated by the economic growth that followed the Civil War. This was at the same time that the last survivors of the generation that had "tamed the wilderness" were passing off the scene. The generation which followed had heard, at their parents' knees, the pioneer accounts. They were in a position of time and influence to romanticize and idealize the pioneer past. During this same era, because of the interest in the past, research was being done, articles were published, and long forgotten documents pulled from the archives and made available to the reading public for the first time. This phenomenon had its effect on Niles.

From the earliest days, farmers along the river bottom south of town had plowed up rusted and broken relics, guns, knives, axes, arrowheads, gunflints, etc. Because they were found in such quantities, the area was assumed to be the location of some long forgotten battle. In the early years it was thought of as junk and treated as such. Later on, local collectors began to comb the ground for relics for their private collections. As the terrace where most of the "junk" was found began to be inundated by the backwaters from the dam, collectors hired local boys to dig and sift the area in a last salvage attempt.

When the Michigan Pioneer Society began to publish the records of the British Regime in the Great Lakes the local historians began to understand that their "old battleground" was the site of Fort Saint Joseph. As they unraveled the story, they began to learn about other "historic" sites in the area, and lest the knowledge of these sites be again forgotten, they marked them with commemorative monuments.

Early relic hunters E. Lombard, E. H. Crane, Hillis Smith, and Lewis Beeson are searching the old fort site for relics after a spring plowing. The collections of Indian artifacts and colonial era relics from the fort area donated by such early "archaeologists" form the basic Fort Saint Joseph artifact collections in the Niles Museum today. The standards and procedures of modern archaeology had not yet been developed so much scientific archaeological information was lost. However these early collectors preserved artifacts that would otherwise have been lost beneath many feet of water and silt.

Fort Saint Joseph Monument

In 1906 the ladies of the Monday Reading Club decided that a monument to perpetuate the memory of the old fort was needed. They did some preliminary research and realized that the resources needed would exceed their capability if a monument of any significance was to be erected. They appealed to the county-wide federation of women's clubs, but met with little interest. They then approached each of the various men's and women's clubs and associations in Niles with the idea. Each of the major organizations selected two representatives who met and formed the Fort Saint Joseph Society in 1910, for the express purpose of creating a monument for the fort.

The committee considered a number of ideas, and decided to place a suitably marked rock as a monument. One of the committeemen located a large rock, that appeared to be about four or five feet in diameter, on the Peter Malone farm about three miles south of town. The committee went out to see the stone and agreed that it was suitable. Mr. Malone was pleased to donate the rock. The French Paper Company gave the Society the land needed for the monument. The Society than began to raise funds for the project with the major anticipated expense being the cost of moving the rock into place. It was difficult to find a contractor who would be willing to undertake the effort involved. Finally, a contractor from South Bend agreed and gave a maximum cost estimate for the project of $400. Agreement was reached and the work began in the fall of 1912 after the ground

The rock in its original setting on the Peter Malone farm with members of the Malone family and the Society.

Loaded onto its gondola for the move.

Placed in its final location preparatory to the pouring of the cement platform. It has been turned upside down. The lower half is the originally exposed portion.

froze. However, it was soon found that the rock was at least three times the size anticipated. It weighed in excess of 65 tons. Moving the monstrous boulder from its forest bed to the nearby railroad tracks, then down the tracks to a point where it could be moved to its final site, proved to be an almost impossible task; physically for the contractor and financially to the Society. But, by Christmas of 1912 the moving was complete, at a cost that more than doubled the initial estimate. The final site work, the cement platform, landscaping, etc., was completed that spring, and a very gala dedication was planned for the upcoming Fourth of July.

FORT ST. JOSEPH DEDICATION OVER

MOST HISTORICAL EVENT HAPPENING IN SOUTHWESTERN MICHIGAN.

HUNDREDS PARTICIPATED

The Fourth of July 1913 dedication drew newspapermen from all over the country, even the Boston newspaper carried an illustrated account. The boulder was known for a while as "the rock that made Niles famous." The 4th of July parade that year was given the fort theme and the unveiling was made part of a spectacular celebration that involved most of the city and many of the surrounding communities.

In later years, the state developed its official historical marker program. One of the first markers was placed near the boulder. The site is listed on both the state and national registers of historic sites.

The Allouez Cross

When the first American settlers arrived in the 1820's, a crude wooden cross stood on the east river bluff about a mile south of town. The local Indians, who maintained the cross, said that it marked the burial place of one of the "black-robes," their term for the Jesuit priests. In the 1840's, local boys, digging around the cross had turned up bits of bone and a few beads and religious medals before they were stopped. (The artifacts were confiscated by a local man who preserved them; they were turned over to the museum by his grandson nearly 100 years later.) The tradition was maintained for years and landowners would put up new crosses as the old ones deteriorated. Around the turn of the century newly available documents made it clear that the long dead black-robe was none other than Jean-Claude Allouez. Allouez was one of the major Jesuit missionaries of the 17th century, and also the founder of the mission in the early 1680's, naming it after St. Joseph.

The Womens Progressive League determined to replace the succession of wooden crosses with a permanent cross. Ownership of the burial site was obtained, and plans were made to erect an 11-foot-tall stone cross. Unfortunately, World War I intervened in their plans and it wasn't until 1918 that work was completed and the monument was dedicated.

Fr. Allouez' burial place, marked with this cross, is on the bluff across the road from the site of the boulder and historic marker commemorating the old French fort, mission, and village.

Cary Mission Marker

The year 1922 marked the centennial anniversary of the founding of the Carey Mission to the Potawatomi Indians. In 1923 the Fort St. Joseph Chapter of the Daughters of the American Revolution erected another boulder as a historical monument. The DAR purchased and erected the stone and bronze plaque that stand on the northeast corner of Phillips Road and Niles-Buchanan Road. This location marks the center of the lands granted to the mission.

STATE HISTORIC MARKERS IN NILES

The State of Michigan established the State Historical Marker Program in 1955 to commemorate sites, persons, or events significant to state or community history. To date eight have been erected within the city limits of Niles though there are more sites eligible for this honor as funds can be located to cover the cost of the program.

Historical marker sites in Niles are:

The Fort Saint Joseph Site

St. Mary's Church

Wesley United Methodist Church

The Ring Lardner House

Trinity Episcopal Church

The H.A. Chapin House & Fort St. Joseph Museum

The Ferry Street School

The Four Flags Hotel

One of the earliest markers in the state was erected near the Fort Saint Joseph boulder in 1957. Shown at the dedication are a group of local historical association members. Left to right: John Burke, Mrs. F. J. Plym, Mrs. H. Smith, Ralph and Mary Ballard, Miss J. Griffin, Sheridan Cook, Dr. Phillip Mason (the State's representative at the dedication ceremony), Mrs. R. Shankland, John Gillette, Janet Evert, and Don Kemeny.

In 1971 the congregation of St. Mary's Church obtained a marker for their historic church. Here Msgr. John Slowey is showing the marker to two of his parishoners.

Chapter II

1829-1848

Pioneers & Progress

THE PIONEER STORY

The settlement pattern of the Four Flags area is different from the stereotypical image of the "pioneer" or "frontiersman" perpetuated by most of the popular print, movie, and electronic media. By the time the "American" settlers arrived here in the late 1820's and the early 1830's many aspects of the wilderness had already been tamed. There had already been an established European community in the area for nearly 150 years. The French had arrived in the 1680's and the English in the 1760's. Though most of the original Fort Saint Joseph community was gone, the few remaining traders and the "metis" or mixed blood Indians preserved its influence. This influence created a social and cultural environment which made peaceful settlement by the American pioneers possible. The Indians had developed an appreciation, indeed a need, for manufactured goods, tools, textiles, and household items which could be obtained only through trade. Previously the need for these items had been met by the traders at the fort. The old trade system began to break down around the end of the 19th century as the British left the area. It is most probable that the first settlers were looked on as harbingers of a revived trade economy in the area by the Indians. It was no coincidence that the so-called "first settler" families (Walling, Justice, and Lacey) set up a general store as their first venture upon arrival in 1828.

The Indians here were considered civilized; at least in that they were Christians by government standards. They had been converted to Catholicism over 150 years previously by the French Jesuit missionaries; and though priestless for the past 50 years, had continued to practice their faith. The government-sponsored mission school, though Baptist rather than Catholic, taught useful domestic and agricultural skills to the local Indians, in addition to basic education and religion. (Religious education was common in almost all schools of that era since Christian virtues were considered to be the basic building blocks of civilized society.) The Potawatomi people themselves, while still following a modified seasonal migration pattern, were primarily an agricultural group operating from a relatively fixed base.

In the St. Joseph River valley (and later the Niles area) there was no need for the stereotypical steely-eyed, buckskin befringed hero — fighting off the savages with one hand while taming the wilderness with the other. In fact, a strong case can be made that the local savages may have been more civilized and had a higher standard of living than some of the first American settlers. It has been reported that after the "removal" of the Indians in the 1830-1840 period, there was fighting in some areas over the right to move into the houses of the evicted Indians, as their French-style log homes were superior to the primitive cabins of the American settlers.

In the 1820's, land in western Michigan became available for settlement and speculation. In an era of rudimentary financial systems and poor communications, land was the one item of lasting and steadily increasing value. Land speculation, buying land cheap when it first became available and selling it later at a profit, fueled much of the economic, political and military activity in the country in the late 18th and early 19th centuries.

Many of the early pioneers in the area arrived here with the idea of profitable land speculation in their minds. A number of the first white men in the area were from relatively wealthy families in the East who came to scout out the best lands and claim them. Often they then returned to the East where whole family groups, sometimes accompanied by friends and neighbors, liquidated all their assets and

This artistic version of a trading post or general store at the turn of the 19th century is probably not too far off the reality experienced by traders like Bertrand, Burnett and the Laceys.

The fringed leather clothing would be more typical of settlers and traders who came up from the southern areas. Those with New England and French backgrounds used more textiles in their garb, as did most of the Indians.

came West. They came to buy up the new cheap land, often platting towns and townships where nothing but trees existed. Soon the highly desirable prairie lands were taken and later arrivals were forced to pay the owners' price or else take up lands in the forest where years of hard labor were required to clear the trees and prepare the land for agriculture.

Under terms of some of the treaties in which the Indians gave over their lands to the government, individual Indians were often granted sizeable sections of land as private reservations. Often these sections were soon sold or traded to speculators. Men like Joseph Bertrand, who had wives who were part Indian, were able to claim private reservations for their wives and their part-Indian children. (Though in Bertrand's case his claim was questionable since his wife Madeline was a part-French part-Canadian Indian *metis* with no legitimate claim to the local lands. The local Indians who had legitimate claims apparently did not protest this, perhaps because of their dependence on Bertrand for supplies and as a reward for his assistance to them in the treaty negotiations).

Joseph Bertrand

Bertrand used the land claimed in his wife and children's name to establish the town of Bertrand, just immediately south of Niles, where he operated a trading post/store and inn.

At first the new settlers were forced to live in temporary cabins and to practice basic subsistence farming because of several limiting factors. Probably the most significant of these was the problem of transportation. While the government had laid out the military road from Fort Dearborn (Chicago) to Detroit it was little more than a blazed track totally unsuited for shipment of bulky products. Lumber, corn and wheat, the major local products, even when milled (another of the limiting problems), were still too bulky and weighty to transport. Prior to development of either a profitable method of shipment or a substantial local market there was little inducement to increase production.

Two major industries evolved to resolve this situation. One was the development of water powered mills for grinding grain (grist mills) and sawmills for reducing the forest to useable and saleable lumber. The other was the development of riverboats of various types to ship bulk cargos down to the lake where they could be loaded onto sailing ships for transport to distant markets. The earliest types were keel or flat boats, but very early on (1832/33) steamboats started to be seen on the river. Once the transportation problem was solved, a cash economy developed which stimulated the importation of luxury goods — at least luxurious in comparison to the more landlocked pioneer settlements.

Settlers came here from several different directions. The first groups came overland following the trail up from Richmond, Indiana, via Fort Wayne to the St. Joseph River near Elk Heart's village, then following the trails downstream to the main ford on the river near the site of the old French settlement. The first settlers had been the staff at the Cary Mission School who came in the 1820's. They were followed by the Walling/Justice/Lacey party, who arrived in 1829 and platted and named the village of Niles in honor of Hezekiah Niles, the editor of a prominent political newspaper of that era. As with the French nearly 150 years previously, the location on the river flats adjacent to the river crossing was an economically attractive place to establish their business and homes. Many of the first wave of pioneers were of southern origin, coming from Virginia, Kentucky, and southern Ohio.

At about this same time the Erie Canal was opened linking New York's Hudson River to the Great Lakes. This opened the way for numbers of New York and other New England immigrants to make their way by canal boat to Buffalo, New York and then by lake boat to the western end of Lake Erie and then overland by ox-drawn wagon to the mid-west. Often these "yankees" were looking for good land to buy for both settlement and speculation. Among them were a high percentage of professional men, doctors, lawyers, teachers etc., who came west to ply their trade as well as to speculate in land. They were unlike some pioneers who arrived with little more than an axe, gun, frying pan, a mule or horse, a cow, and a couple of pigs. Their first shelter may have been little more than a three-sided "half-face" cabin, but it held their heirloom mahogany furniture and their good table linens and silver while they were building their homes. Such primitive conditions were temporary and lasted only until their houses were completed. These houses may have had a log structure, but they were usually covered with sawn boards and built in the fashionable Federal or Greek Revival style.

The Erie Canal also brought another influx of emigrants from the East. These folks were mostly foreign-born. Many Irish had come to the new world to work on the Erie Canal and other similar labor intensive "improvements." Many of them moved west to settle in newly developing areas where their labor was valuable. Conditions of unrest in Europe also resulted in the emigration of large numbers of Germans who came seeking peace, freedom, and security. Substantial numbers of both groups found homes in Niles, the Germanic folk provided many skilled artisans and tradesmen, and the Irish took up work as farmers and laborers. A number of families who had previously taken up lands in southern Indiana sold their partially improved claims to second wave immigrants and moved up to new lands in Michigan.

With the continued influx of Yankees, Germans, Irish, and Hoosiers the population of the Niles area grew from only a dozen or so non-Indians in the late 1820's to over 1400 by 1840. The town continued to grow, and with the arrival of the railroads in 1848 the

THE CAREY MISSION STORY

In response to the Potawatomi Indians requests for educational and religious support, the U.S. Government approved the request of Rev. Isaac McCoy to move his existing Indian Mission School from the Fort Wayne (Indiana) area to a site just west of present day Niles. The school was named after William Carey, the Englishman considered to be the "first foreign missionary." (The Mission's original land grant is roughly quartered by the intersection of Phillips Road and Niles-Buchanan Road.) The school opened in 1820 with a staff of three and about 30 students. It soon grew to an extensive facility with the necessary farms, fields and orchards required to make it pretty much self sufficient, and to provide up-to-date practical education in agricultural and domestic arts to the students. The number of staff grew as well, both in the school teaching and in the practical arts' areas. Among the names of the earliest settlers of the area are many who came here initially as employees of the school.

By 1830 it was determined that the school was to be closed since the government planned to move the Indians west of the Mississippi. Rev. McCoy approved of this, viewing it both as inevitable and to remove the Indians from the negative influence of the incoming settlers and their ever present whisky. He worked to facilitate the move, taking a delegation of local Potawatomi leaders west to pick out good lands and making arrangements to alleviate the hardship and abuses which accompanied the removal of some of the other tribes. Upon closure, the government paid the Baptist Mission Board for the value of the improvements the school had made upon the land. The standing crops were appraised at $641 and the buildings at $5,080, a substantial improvement in ten short years.

In 1823 Rev. McCoy described the school's facilities in a report to one of the missionary journals as follows: "For dwellings we have erected five hewed (hewed square — more work but it resulted in a better building) *log houses.......a blacksmith's shop* (vital to both the school and the surrounding Indians), *kitchen, smokehouse, milkhouse, and a stable. We have fenced 60 acres of land, 40 of which we cultivated last year; the produce of which was about 900 bushels of corn, 100 bushels of potatoes, 2000 cabbages. We hope to cultivate the coming season except for 50 acres of corn and potatoes beside our large garden, and to sow in the fall about 25 acres of wheat. Hay for our stock is procured on the extensive prairies around us. We have 6 horses, about 175 head of cattle, 80 sheep, and 90 hogs. We have as yet, no mill to grind our grain* (an ox powered mill was soon built), *and no house for the female department of our school; which is currently taught in one of the dwelling houses."*

Reverend Issac McCoy

Christiana McCoy

32

Though the majority of the Potawatomi Indians were moved to new lands in the Kansas and Oklahoma territories, one small group was allowed to remain here in southwest Michigan. Many of the tribe avoided the deportation by fleeing into the woods, becoming refugees among other tribes in northern Michigan and Wisconson, or escaping to Canada. Several hundred, under the leadership of men like Leopold Pokagon, Wesaw, Topash and others, found legal means to stay in their homelands.

One of the reasons they were able to do so was because of their religious status. Because they were recognized as Christians (Roman Catholic), they were given special status. They also either had (or were in the process of) acquiring land for their band in the recognized U.S. government approved manner — by buying it back from the government with funds from the treaty settlement. Though they have moved several times within the area and have suffered much over the years, there still is a large group of several thousand Potawatomi residing in the area. Most of them trace their ancestry to members of the *Pokagon Band,* as the Catholic Potawatomi are called.

Topenibe, (commonly called Young Topenibe since his influential father had the same name) became one of the leaders of the portion of the Potawatomi who emigrated west in the 1830's. (Photo courtesy of Northern Indiana Historical Society)

Leopold Pokagon, a Chippewa assimilated into the Potawatomi tribe, married into the family of Topenibe Sr. He gradually grew to be very influential among the tribe and became the leader of the Catholic portion of the tribe which stayed in the area. He was pro-American and a strong supporter of the Carey Mission in its early days, though he came to differ with the McCoys over the removal issue. (Photo courtesy of Northern Indiana Historical Society)

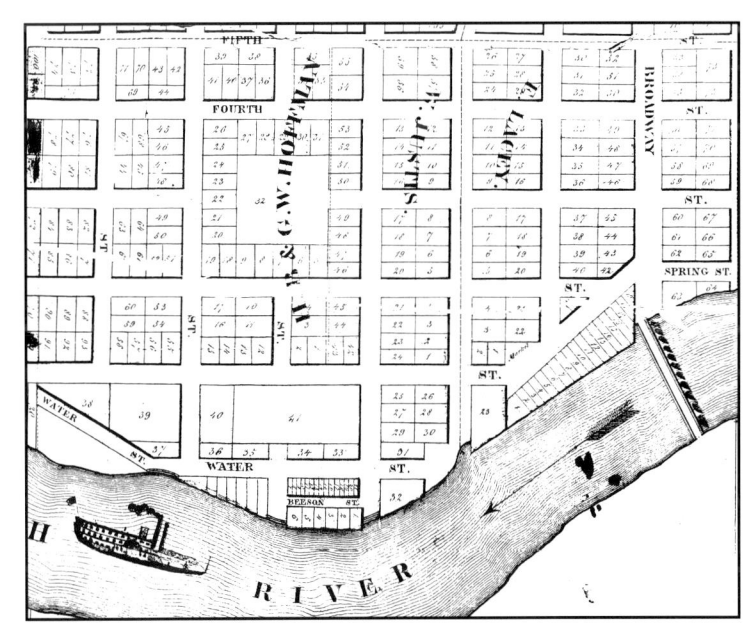

This 1837 plat map shows the layout of the platted area of Niles. Since plat maps were often sales tools to help market the platted property they often show "improvements," (like the riverboat and the combination bridge and dam at the foot of Broadway) that were still in the planning stages, as realities.

Keelboats such as this artist's interpretation provided most of the early pioneer period river transportation.

EARLY RIVER TRAVEL

After the collapse of the fur trade, use of the river as an avenue of commerce pretty well subsided until the late 1820's. The earliest settlers had little to ship to market, but as the area developed, so did the river traffic. Flatboats and "arks" were put together using the locally produced lumber in upstream towns and villages and loaded with local products such as wheat, corn, lumber or shingles, as well as barrels of locally made whiskey and salted down meat. These raft type barges were then floated down to the mouth of the river where the cargos would be sold and the craft broken up for the lumber and sold as well. The crews would have to walk home. Keelboats, as pictured in this artist's interpretation (above), were an improvement in that they were designed to make repeated round trips. They could be drifted, oared, sailed and poled. The keelboatmen were a colorful and vigorous lot, and Niles in the 1830's and early '40's was known as a riverboat town, with all that that included. At least one early missionary preacher felt that the behavior of boatmen put Niles into the ranks of Biblical Sodom and Gomorrah. But, he had just had the experience of having all the men in his congregation get up and walk out of the service when the horn signaling the arrival of a riverboat sounded during a Sunday morning service.

Excerpted from the pages of the *Niles Republican* and written by its editor:

"Having never had a ride on a steamer to St. Joseph, on Monday last, with our better half and two of our young responsibilities, we boarded the steamer *John F. Porter*, Capt. Gorham (commanding), and embarked down the river. It was a beautiful day, but the sun showed us little mercy. Down we steamed, stopping here and there to take in wood, and occasionally picking up a passenger who gave a signal from the river bank. It seems these steamers have no regular stopping places, but will pick up a passenger wherever they hail them, or to take on freight. At Buchanan, we received quite an accession in our company — Mr. Bradley, from Three Oaks, Mr. Partridge, from Chickaming, Mr. Stratton, from New Buffalo, Mr. Clark, from Buchanan, all Supervisors, on their way to Berrien. (Editor: The County Board of Supervisors met in Berrien Springs which was the County seat at that time.) "Arriving at Berrien, about fifty men belonging to a rifle company (Editor: this occurred during the Civil War) got on board. Some were from Dowagiac, some from Berrien. This company was on their way to Chicago to join the Douglas Brigade. We now had music in abundance. They were a fine looking body of men, most of them quite young. Their Captain spent considerable time on the way down in drilling them."

The first steamboat appeared on the river in 1832. However it was a brief appearance since her design was not compatible with the shallow twisting channel of the river. It wasn't until the late 1830's that steamboats became a major factor in local commerce. The first steamers were sternwheelers, but soon two side mounted paddle wheels (as shown here on the *John F. Porter*) were adopted as the standard drive system because they were much more maneuverable in the tight and twisting river channels. By driving one side wheel forward and reversing the other, the ship could turn 180 degrees within its own length.

The *May Graham* is the best remembered of the St. Joseph riverboats (probably because she is the only one people still alive can remember). While she originally traveled much farther up the river, construction of dams at Niles, Buchanan, and Berrien Springs, eventually restricted her to the lower river between Berrien Springs and Lake Michigan. She was the last commercial steamboat on the river, making her last run in 1911. After that she was transferred to the Grand River where she worked until 1918 when she was disassembled for scrap.

The *May Graham* and many other river steamers like her plied the river in the last half of the 19th century carrying fruit, general cargo, and passengers. These flatbottomed riverboats were surprisingly large. (The *May Graham* was 116 feet in length and 22 feet wide.) They were reputed to be able to "travel on a heavy dew" since they were of extremely shallow draft, capable of traveling in water little more than two or three feet deep. On their trips upstream they carried loads of merchandise or supplies for farms and businesses along the river. On their trip back downstream, produce from fields and farms was the usual cargo.

Passenger service was an equally important factor with as many as 150 of them carried on a boat like the *May Graham* for an excursion cruise to the parks and resorts along the river. Often keelboats or barges filled with an additional 150 or 200 passengers were towed behind or beside on special trips. The *Nettie June,* one of the smaller excursion boats on the river, is shown here in a circa 1890 photo with a keelboat full of passengers fastened alongside. Many visitors from Chicago and Milwaukee came over on the lake boats and transferred to the riverboats to get to the summer resorts along the river. This tourist passenger traffic was especially important in the 1880's and '90's.

In addition to the commercial boats on the river there were a large number of smaller boats used for pleasure and recreation. Illustrated is the private steam launch of the Lardner family. Many wealthy people had similar elegant launches which were used for picnic trips to islands in the river, fishing excursions, or just plain relaxing cruises on hot summer evenings. A number of them were docked at private piers and boathouses on the river in the downtown area. Many other folk had various rowboats, canoes, or scows, for hunting and fishing or simply to get from one side of the river to the other.

Dams and Mills

Processing of grain into edible meal has always been one of man's vital concerns. The Indians used mortars and pestles to grind their corn. One of the important activities at Rev. McCoy's Carey Mission was the operation of an animal powered grinding mill for the Indians and the mission staff. With the arrival of the other early pioneers in the late 1820's, the building of water powered mills had a very high priority. Sawmills for converting logs into boards and planks for construction were also a critical necessity for settlement. A grist mill and a sawmill were established on the Dowagiac Creek about 1830. Other water powered mills were built on that stream in later years.

Mills had to be located where proper water volume and speed as well as the right soil conditions existed. Sometimes the location of the mills were not convenient to the settlements; and early accounts tell of pioneer settlers carrying grain or hauling logs for many miles to get them processed. (The early Niles' settlers had to travel up the hill from the river banks to the trail that is now Fifth Street and go north about a mile, then back down the bluff, to get to their mills.) The availability of mills was one of the two conditions (along with a reliable means of transportation) that was needed to make agriculture profitable to the early American settlers of the area. The streams and rivers once dammed and harnessed, provided power for many types of early industrial developments.

While putting a dam across a creek or stream was a sizeable undertaking, it was usually done under the direction of an experienced mill builder, who often was also the mill owner and operator. He often had the willing help of the area farmers who would benefit from the mill.

However, damming the St. Joseph River was an entirely different story. From the earliest times it had been a desirable improvement and the necessary legal work was done in the 1830's. An attempt was made in the 1840's by a committee of local businessmen. They raised the money, developed a plan for a dam with locks for shipping, and hired the contractors. The dam was built on the site of the present Main Street bridge. Unfortunately, the partially completed dam was washed away in the flood of 1843, and the project was abandoned. It would be another 30 years before the river would be harnessed.

Steam engines, which became available in the 1830's, never completely replaced water power as an industrial power source. In 1871, a corporation was formed for the purpose of building a dam on the river and selling industrial building sites with the right to the water power generated by the dam. This project, when successfully completed, was the first planned industrial development in Niles, and could be considered our first industrial park.

This mill on the Pokagon Creek started out as a sawmill in the 1840's; was converted to wool processing in the 1860's; and later into a grain grinding mill or feed mill. It burned in 1884.

Not all mills needed dams. Some including the Volant Mill stood on the river bank and had wheels that ran directly in the river current. The Volant was one of three mills that were located at the foot of Pokagon Street. It was believed to have been built in the 1830's and operated up to the 1930's when it was destroyed in a fire. In its later years it was a feed mill and the equipment was operated by electricity.

Early dam construction was a major community project. In the foreground are the timbers for one of the mill races. In the left foreground is the pile-driver used to drive the timbers into the ground. This is almost certainly a photo of the construction crew who built the 1871 dam on the river.

The timber and earth dam had a wooden sheath to protect it from water erosion. In the background are the head gates on the east bank of the river where water entered the mill race.

Twenty years later the timber and earth dam was replaced with a concrete structure. Wooden riser boards were added to give increased water power to the mills. A steam powered pile-driver is shown on temporary tracks on top of the dam for driving the supports for the riser boards.

This bird's-eye view drawing shows the dam and the mills on either side of the river as they appeared in 1889. Water from the mill race passed through brick tunnels under the spinning mill wheels to provide the power. Originally, the mills on the near bank (the east side of the river) were three separate factories. Later they were incorporated into the Ohio Paper Company. The factory on the west bank was also a paper mill.

> Miss Lizzie Dutch, of Niles, has worked ten years in the paper mill at that place, boarding with her parents on the opposite side of the river, and there being no bridge at that point she kept a boat and rowed herself across the river on an average of four times a day. Allowing 300 working days in a year she has rowed herself across twelve thousand times. All praise to Lizzie.

Clipped from the *Niles Mirror* June 1883.

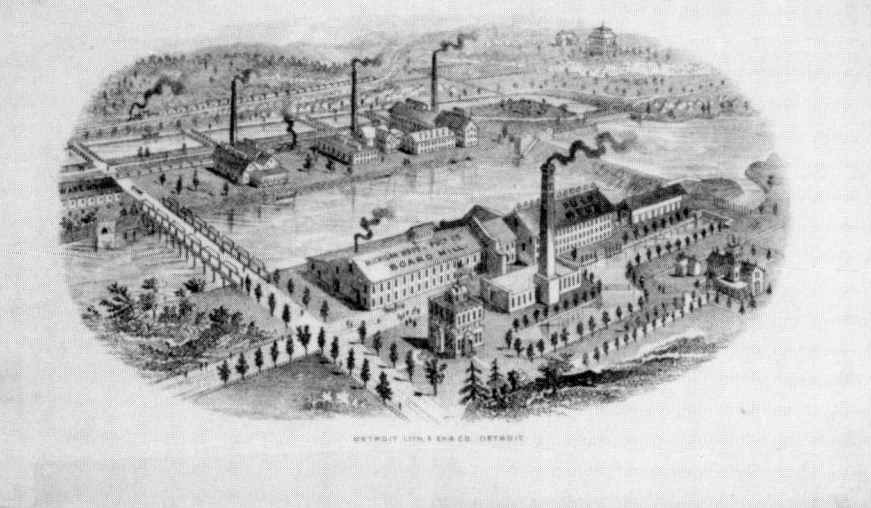

This Michigan Wood Pulp Company business card from the late 1870's shows its assets, products and management on one side and a bird's-eye view of the industrial complex on the other.

39

The office staff of the French Paper Company circa 1895. The man in the hat is J.W. French.

In the 1880's J. W. French bought out the Millards and in 1904 changed the name from the Michigan Wood Pulp Company to The French Paper Company With four generations of the French family involved in the management of the company, French Paper Company is not only Niles' oldest business but it is the oldest family owned and operated business in the state.

After the Chapins bought the Ohio Paper Mills (everyone continued to use the old name) they were struck with a series of disastrous fires. One of the three mills burned in 1902, another in 1914, the third was closed in 1915. The burned out ruins were demolished and for many years the site was used as the town dump. As a 1976 Bi-Centennial project the site was improved to become part of the Riverfront Park.

The major product of the Niles Board & Paper Company was a type of cardboard and a coarse wrapping paper for the meat processing industry. These products were made from straw which was purchased from local farmers. In this picture a large pile of straw is visible at the extreme right. The road between the straw stack and the mill race is now Bond Street. The foundations of these factories still stand in Riverfront Park where the parking lot is located on the filled-in millrace.

41

One of the earliest known street photos shows Niles as it looked at the end of the Civil war. This view, dated 1870, looks uphill on Main from the east river bank.

While dating from a generation or so later this shows the Main Street scene still relatively unchanged — except for the addition of the wooden utility poles. This May 31, 1898 photo shows a large number of flags on display for Memorial Day.

Chapter III

1848 – 1890

Era of Transition

In the previously described era, (the pioneer or settler period of the 1820's, '30's and early '40's) the main economic base of the community was agriculture. What few industries existed (if you wished to classify them as industries) did so primarily to serve the farmers' needs. These were of course the early mills and the riverboat building trade. This next period in the history of Niles was an era of transition from the pioneer community to an industrial town. While agriculture continued to play a large role in the economy and lifestyle of the community, industry and manufacturing gradually became the major economic base of the town. These changes did not occur abruptly in 1848, nor did they end suddenly in 1890. Niles became an industrial town over a period of generations in a process of development that saw changes in almost every aspect of the community.

The selection of 1848 as a watershed year is an arbitrary choice based on a specific significant event — the advent of the railroad in Niles. To pick such a specific event, perhaps risks assigning too much emphasis to a single phenomenon since history is a complex flow of events, personalities and circumstances working in interrelationship. There were indeed many other causes and effects at work in the community; but the arrival of the first train symbolizes the beginning of the era of transition most conveniently.

This period was a time of change for the whole country as well as an age of invention and innovation, of significant social change, of evolution in the national character, and of course it was the period of the Civil War. The innovations of the era all had an impact on the community. Many inventions which improved agricultural and industrial productivity or helped increase the speed and reliability of transportation and communication were to be found in use in Niles. A number of them were invented and manufactured here in the region.

One of the most significant changes, of course, were the railroads. With their advent the geographic location of the community between the industry/capital centers of the East and the rapidly expanding markets of the Midwest and Trans-Mississippi West became advantageous for business. The railroads brought in new emigrants, fresh ideas, and more capital. Even more important was the increased importation of raw materials and the exportation of finished products. As it had been for the previous century and a half, the key to the community's success was its location.

Another significant change was the increased use of steam power in industrial settings; thus converting the forest from an obstacle to settlement to a source for fuel and raw material. While water power remained the major source of industrial power, (indeed one of the major local accomplishments of the era was the successful damming of the river in 1871 for Niles' first industrial park) the stationary steam mills provided the muscle for manufacturing facilities which were not located on streams or rivers.

Not all of the changes were of a technological nature, however. One of the problems of the previous era was the lack of a stable financial system to supply, transfer, and manage the capital which financed these new ventures. The collapse of the independent "wildcat" banks in the 1830's had almost destroyed the pioneer settlements in that era. Now banks and financial institutions were developed and controlled in such a way as to restore the public confidence. Development could proceed with a reasonable assurance that the financial systems would be reliable enough to support them.

At the time these changes were occurring in North America, major economic and military upheavals were also taking place in northern Europe. As a result, many skilled European tradesmen and farmers emigrated to America seeking economic and political freedom as well as to avoid compulsory military service. This new wave of highly motivated and skilled workers helped fuel the industrialization of Niles and the rest of America. Many of the ancestors of today's residents arrived at this time.

This era of transition saw the beginning of modern-day Niles in that the community which had been organized as a village in the 1830's was rechartered as a city in 1859, with a government system which remained relatively unchanged for the next century and a quarter. As the community grew in size and complexity it became apparent that the "ad hoc" informal pioneer manner of dealing with community security and safety no longer met the town's needs. It was during this period that the fire, police, and public service departments had their beginnings as government services.

The stimulus provided by the Civil War's requirements for men and material furthered the development of the local industries as both industry and agriculture produced food and equipment for the military effort. The war also had a social and cultural impact on the local community. The local population was divided over the issues at stake as is reflected in the newspapers of the time. As men went off to war women assumed a greater role in the economic life of the community by filling the need for "manpower" in town and on the farm.

It was in this period that Niles incorporated its school system and began making the steps needed to advance beyond the primitive settler schools. The Union School and the first high school were products of this era. They helped create a more literate and knowledgeable populace which, in turn, helped create a more skilled, more efficient workforce.

While medical knowledge was still rudimentary by today's standards, it was vastly improved over that of the preceding generations. Niles residents could be assured of the best that the medical arts had to offer.

On the spiritual side, Niles made considerable improvements in this era as well. Many of the churches now in existence began in this period. A substantial number of them in buildings built at that time.

By 1860 Niles' population had grown to nearly 2,800. In the next ten years it increased to 4,650 then dropped slightly, holding fairly steady in the 4,000 range for the rest of the century. During these same years, the value of the city as it was expressed in the tax evaluations jumped from an 1860 value of $918,000 to $1,700,000 by 1870 (thus nearly doubling), and then slowly growing to $2,000,000 by the end of the century. Once past the initial increase in population in the first years of this era of transition (which resulted in increased valuation because of new housing) the remainder of the increase in value was largely due to the development of Niles' industries.

A view south on Front Street from Sycamore showing the *Niles Daily Sun* newspaper building, which is still standing, in the foreground on the west side of the street.

This late 1800's photo shows Main Street in its original unpaved condition with open gutters. Cobblestone and plank crosswalks were an effort to keep pedestrians' feet out of the mud and other grime. Both carbon arc and gaslamps are clearly visible.

THE CIVIL WAR

The Civil War was a major trauma for Niles, just as it was for the rest of the country. The stress on the community caused by the intense feelings over the issues of slavery and states' rights were complicated by other local and regional issues. Because many of the early settlers had come from the South and a substantial number of others had Quaker or New England backgrounds, popular opinion was very divided. Both the "underground railroad" and the "copperheads" had supporters in the local area (though the former was exaggerated and the latter denied — after the war was over). Both abolitionist and anti-abolitionist views could be found in the local papers. Both positions probably represented extremely vocal and visible minorities, the majority were then, as now, probably more concerned with local issues.

Once the war actually began, the major issue at stake was states' rights, and the legality of secession. While the question of slavery was a real controversy, it is probable that most of the 3,100 plus Berrien County men who enlisted did so to preserve the Union rather than to free the slaves.

A recruitment camp known as Camp Barker was set up on the County Fairgrounds shown above (which was then located on the west side of South 11th Street across from the cemetery) in Niles for the 12th Michigan Infantry Regiment. Well over half this unit was made up of men from the local area. The enlistees received their basic training there between October of 1861 and March of 1862. Then they were shipped by train (all 1000 officers and men) to St. Louis. Within a matter of weeks they received their baptism of fire on the battlefield of Shiloh (also known as Pittsburgh Landing). Of the men from the 12th Michigan, 40 were killed and 80 were wounded.

Eli Griffin

Noah Cain

Hoel Wright

Two of Niles' finest. A popular man-about-town, Eli Griffin's enlistment inspired many other young men to join and serve. Noah Cain was another young volunteer from Niles, barely out of his youth. Both men gave their all, victims of the Civil War, representatives of a whole generation. Hoel Wright, who joined Dygert's Sharpshooters (16th Infantry) was one of the men who came back.

The Union veterans of the Civil War formed an organization known as the Grand Army of the Republic to represent their needs to the government for pensions and other veteran's benefits. Portrayed in this 1907 photo are the three surviving members of the Niles' G.A.R. riding in the back of Bascom Parker's Ford. They were Steven Moore, John Hatfield, and D. D. Robinson.

Niles physician Dr. Evan J. Bonine (father of F.N. Bonine, the famous eye doctor) was appointed regimental surgeon for the 2nd Regiment of the Michigan Infantry in 1862. After the Medical Service was reorganized and federalized later in the war, he was placed in charge of the 3rd Division/9th Corps (Burnsides) medical service where he was division surgeon and chief operator. In this 1864 photo Dr. Bonine, seated center front, posed with the division surgical staff during the seige of Petersburg.

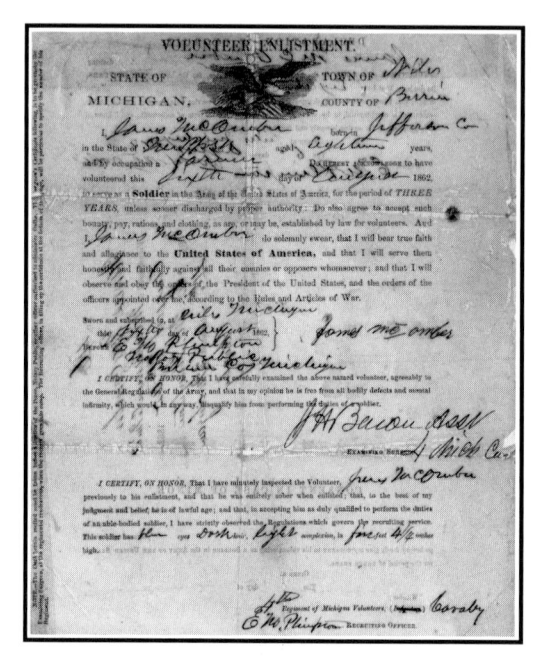

1862 enlistment paper of James McComber of Niles in the 4th Michigan Cavalry Regiment

During the Civil War the economy of the whole area was mobilized and invigorated. The need to equip and supply the army was aggravated by crop failures, notably wheat and hops, in other parts of the country. Local farmers (and millers like G.A. Colby who became known as the "cracker-king" and built the Castle Rest mansion) made extensive profits from the local harvests. Flour was used to make "hardtack" the oversize triple-baked cracker-like biscuit which was the mainstay of the army's field ration and the bane of the soldier's teeth. The piece of hardtack shown here is an actual Civil War ration from the Fort Saint Joseph Museum's collections

ON THE HOME FRONT

The war's impact on Niles was in two major areas, which in turn affected others. First was the loss of manpower in the labor force. In those early years of the machine age, both agriculture and industry (the major employment areas) were still very labor intensive. In 1860 the whole county had a total population of 22,500, according to the census figures. The temporary loss of 3,100 men in their prime working years, represented a tremendous loss in productivity. At the same time, the needs for materials with which to make war, munitions obviously, but also, clothing (uniforms), food supplies, wagons, horses and mules, increased drastically. These latter products were also needed by the civilian population as well. The competing civilian and military requirements fueled major changes in the local as well as the national economy.

Another major change was the entry of women into the labor force. While women had always been present to some degree, the loss of manpower made the woman's role more visible. Women now were forced, in some cases, to operate farms without adult male help, and to work for wages in industries which had been male dominated.

Though they had been invented some years earlier the war made the sewing machine a popular item, first as a way of mass producing the millions of uniforms needed and later for the general public. One of the first in Niles was used by the wife of Dr. E. J. Bonine to make his non-issue clothing. However, most of the wives and daughters continued to sew by hand since the sewing machines, while desirable, were too expensive for the average household until after the war. This engraving is from a Civil War era advertisement for Grover & Baker sewing machines.

So first you boil and then cool, then drain. Scrub it well and add, with onion, to boiling water. then cook till claws can be taken. Drain again and take away shell and gall. Save liver and eggs for later. Take meat in pot and cover two times with water and beef stock, whole celery, salt, butter, flour, and spices. Chop and add small intestines. Now add liver and eggs. Cook til done, so then eat.

During the the Civil War, turtle soup was more than just a popular soup. Culinary battles raged over who had the best turtle or "terripen" recipe. Some felt the French version was superior to the British while both the North and the South championed their regional recipe. While the wealthy argued, the slaves of the Tidewater plantations were said to be complaining of the constant daily diet of turtle soup there. Here in Niles a brief excursion to the cool clean Saint Joseph River could easily bring home a turtle for a heartily enjoyed dinner of turtle soup.

An adaptation of this Civil War era reciept offers an opportunity to savor this much sought after delicacy.

Churches

Niles has a long history of religious institutions. The very first European residents were the Jesuit priests. Under the leadership of Father Jean-Claude Allouez they established the Mission of Saint Joseph for the Indians in the early 1680's. This Mission existed until the 1780's. Local traditions say that the chapel building was moved to Bertrand and that it later was moved to South Bend where Father Sorin used it to start what is now the University of Notre Dame.

The Potawatomi Indians proved to be devout and faithful Catholics. Even after the mission was closed and the priests were withdrawn they continued to preserve their religious traditions. They built their own chapel on the banks of the river near one of their main villages, and appealed to the U.S. Government to send a priest to pastor them.

The government, in its wisdom, sent the Reverend Isaac McCoy and his wife Christiana (Baptist missionaries) to start up an Indian school. This school, Carey Mission, which opened in 1822, provided basic education, Protestant religious instruction, and practical teaching in agriculture, animal husbandry, and domestic arts.

The Michigan frontier in the 1820's and 1830's was considered a mission field to the churches in the East. They sent missionary preachers to Niles from various denominations during the early years. Often the early

An interior view of the 1879-1966 Baptist Church ornately decorated, perhaps for Easter, about 1891.

The Baptists formed a congregation in 1841 and erected their first church in 1843. This, their second church was built in 1879 at the corner of 4th and Broadway. It was razed in 1966.

congregations met in homes or in public halls or even taverns. On occasions members of different denominations met together to share facilities and pastors until their own churches were built.

As the community grew the churches did as well, both in size and in number. When the different immigrant groups—Irish, German, etc—arrived in the community, they often established churches that reflected their cultural heritage. Some of Niles' oldest churches were founded in this way.

Church functions, Sunday School activities, ladies' guilds, and church socials, as well as regular church services provided much of the social and cultural life in the community in its early years.

Methodists were among the first in Niles to organize. They had a missionary pastor here in 1829, held the first Sunday School in 1831, and formed the Niles Methodist Episcopal Church in 1832. Their first church building was dedicated on Christmas day in 1839. By 1840 there were over 100 members. It was replaced with this brick edifice in 1862. The African-American community organized an African-Methodist church in 1888.

In 1834 the Presbyterian congregation was organized, and built its first church in 1837. The group later built this white frame edifice in 1850. The "Manse" (pastor's residence) is the white house shown next door These structurs were replaced in 1915 with the Chapin Memorial Church. Today it is known as the First Presbyterian Church of Niles.

In 1934 the Presbyterians celebrated the centennial of their church in Niles with a pageant.

The German United Evangelical Church was formed in 1860. Their first church, this white frame structure, was built on the corner of 6th and Sycamore.

The "new" German church, a brick edifice was erected to replace the old wooden one in 1899 at the cost of $13,000.

The interior of the 1899 German church as it appeared at its dedication. Today this church is known as St. Johns United Church of Christ.

The Catholic settlers of early Niles had to attend services in the little village of Bertrand a few miles south of Niles. A log church was built there in 1831. It was replaced with this brick building in 1837. This church was abandoned in later years when the first Catholic church in Niles was built. The long-abandoned Bertrand Church was photographed prior to its demolition in 1909.

After meeting in Bertrand for a number of years a Catholic church was organized and built in Niles in 1847. The first church, St. Francis of Asissi, was a frame building. The cornerstone of the existing brick church, (now known as St. Mary's Church), was laid in 1862 and it was finished in 1870.

Father John Cappon was in charge of the Niles Catholic congregation from 1859 until his death in 1892. He oversaw the construction of St. Mary's Church and also the establishment of the Catholic school investing much of his personal family fortune in the two projects.

53

The Episcopal congregation was formed in 1834, making it the oldest in the Western Michigan Diocese. Their first building was erected in 1836. It was replaced with this brick church in 1856. The church home was dedicated by Reverend Joseph F. Phillips, maternal grandfather of Ringold "Ring" Lardner, the famous American writer.

The Evangelical Association Church organized in 1904. They dedicated this church on the southeast corner of Grant and Lincoln in 1906. It was replaced with a modern church across the street in 1953. The name was changed to the Evangelical United Brethren Church and later when they merged with the Methodist denomination, it became Grace United Methodist Church.

TRAINS

When the Michigan Central train arrived in Niles at 5 p.m. on October 2, 1848, it was a momentous occasion for the community.

Ten years previously the state legislature had authorized construction of three railroads which would cross the state. The intervening years had seen land speculation, bankruptcy, graft, and failure — in short everything but the railroads. Competition was fierce among pioneer settlements to get the railroads to run through their town. The railroad meant financial success to the towns who got one, and stagnation or worse to those who didn't. Though Niles had the advantage of river access to shipping, the railroads were viewed as economic salvation. Bertrand, the community immediately south of Niles (and a competitor for the railroad), failed in their bid because land speculators had set the prices too high. Consequently the majority of businesses there soon moved to Niles and eventually Bertrand became a "ghost town."

When that first train arrived from Detroit via the Michigan Central Railroad the whole town turned out to greet it. *"At five o'clock the train hove in sight and the cry was raised 'the cars!! the cars!!* (at that time trains were referred to as "cars") *and at almost the same instant they were in front of the depot and were received with three cheers and the music of the Niles Brass Band. Rain was pouring down at the time in torrents and the pealing thunders of artillery of heaven mingled with the din of a thousand voices."* Speeches were made by politicians and railroad officials and the crowd responded with *"nine hearty cheers from the vast assembly."* (Contemporary newspaper account)

At that time, Niles was the end of the line, because the railroad bridge across the river had yet to be built and the track from Niles to Chicago was yet to be laid. A "through ticket" from New York to Chicago carried one as far as Niles by train, then a short livery wagon ride down the hill to the river, then onto a riverboat for a ride to the river's mouth, then a lake ship for the rest of the trip to Chicago. A roundhouse and turntable were built on the top up the bluff (just north of the present tracks between 3rd and Dey streets) to turn the trains around and head them back. The depot itself stood in the area on the northwest corner of the present tracks and 5th Street.

Late the next year, the line was finished to New Buffalo and the direct connection with lake shipping made the inconvenient trip down the river unneces-

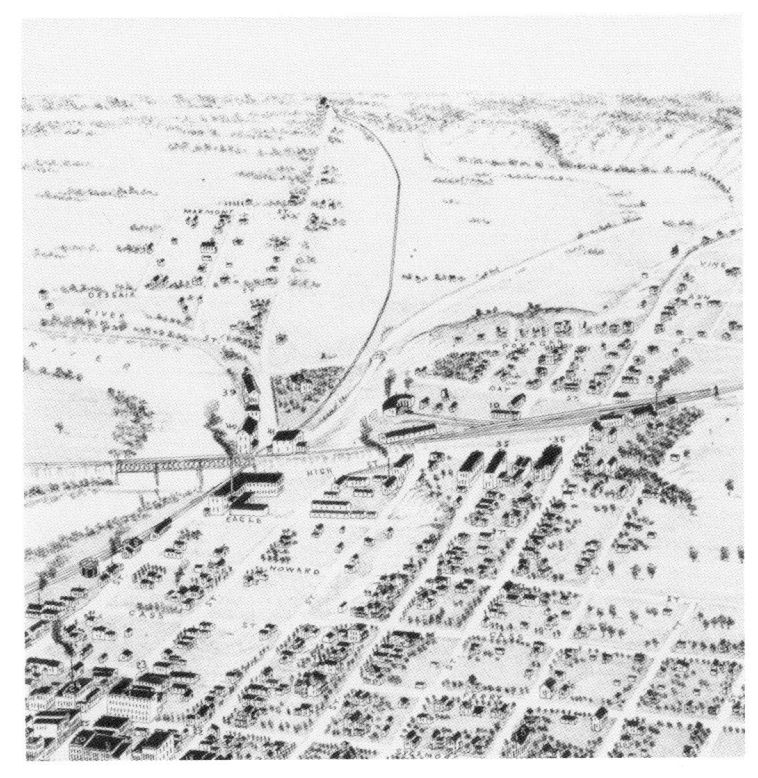

This section of the 1889 bird's-eye-view map shows the railroad business area of early Niles. Most easily recognizable is the round house, between it and the tracks is a freight station, to the east and indicated with a numeral 10 is the first Michigan Central Depot at the corner of 4th Street on the north side of the tracks. On the south side of the tracks are several hotels restaurants and other businesses that catered to the railroad community. Between Front Street and the river (south of the MCRR bridge) are the depot, freight house and water tank of the Big Four railroad.

The original 1848 depot was located at 5th Street and the tracks. It burned down in 1878 and this building at 4th Street and the tracks was used as the depot. It contained the ticket offices, waiting room and a restaurant. In 1891 it was replaced by the present depot.

sary. Because good rail connections provided relatively cheap shipping costs, manufacturing businesses in Niles boomed. This ushered in an era of prosperity which lasted for nearly a hundred years. Inexpensive passenger fares brought many new emigrants to this area and the frequency of passenger trains (18 a day stopped in Niles in 1876) made travel convenient and cheap for everyone. Good transportation, water power, plenty of raw resources, and a large, highly skilled and motivated labor force attracted new businesses and the capital required to make them work.

By the 1880's the Michigan Central traffic in Niles had far outgrown the old depot and a new depot was built. It was designed specifically to be opened just in time for the Columbian Exposition (as the 1892/93 Chicago World's Fair was called). This new elegant depot was built of rose-colored sandstone in the architectural style known as "Richardsonian Romanesque." It had extensive ornamental gardens and greenhouses which provided fresh flowers for all of the MCRR's needs. With the lovely gardens and its new depot, which contained an elegant restaurant, Niles gained an enviable reputation as the "Garden City" among the many thousands of East Coast visitors who passed through on their way to the fair.

Though the Michigan Central was the major railroad, there were other railroads in Niles as well. In 1870 a new route was laid which connected South Bend, Indiana, with Detroit via Niles and Jackson, Michigan. This was known as the Air Line and was built to offer competition to the MCRR through the southern part of the state. However, within a few years of its construction it was absorbed into the MCRR system.

In the late 1870's and early 1880's another railroad began to serve Niles as well. The MCRR was basically an east-west route, so the *Cincinnati, Wabash,* and *Michigan Railway* built a track which ran north and south through Niles. It connected the city with South Bend and towns farther north along the lakeshore, including the county seat. This track ran along the river bank through the downtown area with its own depot on Front Street just south of the MCRR viaduct. This railroad was later taken over by the Big Four which offered many daily trains and was used extensively by excursionists from Indiana seeking relief from the summer heat at the lake's shore. One old account describes them passing through Niles bound for the beach in the morning "all spruced up with clean shirts, starched collars, and shining faces, on the return trip in the evening, they were a bedraggled-looking lot." There were a number of livery services which specialized in carrying passengers and freight between the two depots in

It is believed that this undated photograph shows the flag raising which was part of the grand opening ceremonies for the new depot. Note the landscaped gardens which line both sides of Dey Street and the very early locomotive just visible in the lower right.

order to make connections. The daily train which left Niles at 7:30 a.m. for the county seat and returned at 5:30 p.m., often carried a load of lawyers, jurors, plaintiffs, and defendants. It was known locally as the "Courthouse Flyer."

Along with the MCRR, the Big Four carried a tremendous amount of seasonal fruit and produce from this area to the big city markets. The Big Four alone hauled over 100 cars of fruit a day through Niles, as late as the 1920's. The early refrigerator fruit cars were literally packed with fruit, and ice to keep the fruit fresh. Barron Lake, a popular resort area, was the source of the ice until a large synthetic ice plant was built near the rail yards. In those days its water was considered to be unusually pure. During the winter many men found seasonal work cutting the ice from the frozen surface of the lake and storing it into one of several icehouses. It was layered in sawdust for insulated storage and for later sale to the railroads and for local consumption. The combination of railroad transportation, availability of large quantities of ice, and the unique moderate climate of Southwest Michigan created a tremendous growth in the agricultural economy of the area, which became known as the "Fruit Belt."

In the early years of the 20th century the MCRR made a decision which was to have a tremendous impact on the City of Niles. Up until that time, their train classification yard (where trains were disassembled and cars headed for common destinations reassembled into new trains) was located along the lakeshore, near Michigan City, Indiana, and was their main locomotive and car repair facility. These facilities were getting too old and they were located improperly for maximum efficiency. So the decision was made to move the whole facility to the Niles area.

An extensive area of land on the northeast corner of town was purchased from a very reluctant farmer and in 1918 work began on the massive construction project. Eventually an excess of four million dollars was spent on the facility. When it was completed some years later, it had both an east and a west-bound classification yard with a large man-made hill or "hump" which used gravity to coast the cars onto the appropriate track for sorting. It also included a large car repair yard and building, a 30-stall engine house and turntable, a complete locomotive repair shop (actually a factory capable of building or rebuilding a locomotive from the ground up), office buildings, a 600-ton coaling station, oil houses, and a large hotel for the use of railroad workers.

The transfer of the yards to Niles involved the relocation of nearly 600 MCRR employees from the Michigan City area to Niles as well. The relatively sudden influx of over 400 new families had a real impact on the community of 7000. A housing boom was one of the results. A new section of town, called Eastlake Terrace was developed for them in the area closest to the new railroad facilities. This was done largely with the funds invested for that purpose, in a local building and loan association by John and Horace Dodge (Niles' natives who had become very wealthy as automobile manufacturers). In addition, the sudden increase of new students taxed the capacity of the relatively new high school. Consequently another new school had to be built and older neighborhood schools expanded. The new payrolls and the radically increased expenditure in the area by the railroads for all the construction caused a

Near the old passenger depot on the MCRR line (west of 5th Street) there were several freight buildings. This glass plate image shows some of the freight house workers posing for the photographer around the turn of the century. Wooden kegs, such as these shown stacked on the platform, were a common way of shipping quantities of small hardware items.

major beneficial impact on the economic life of the community—almost all the businesses in town flourished.

Between 1928 and the end of World War II, the Niles yards and related railroad employment reached a peak of almost 1600. During the war years especially, the amount of freight handled in the yards exceeded anything the line had ever experienced. During those peak years Niles was seldom without the sound of trains, day or night.

During World War II, the New York Central Railroad began to acquire stock in MCRR and by 1935 was able to take control and force a merger. Changing from the "M.C." to "N.Y.C." was painful to many. Generations of railroaders had grown up working for the M.C. and hated to take off their old M.C. uniform badges and put on those of the rival N.Y.C.

But that pain was nothing to that felt by the next generation, when in 1957 the N.Y.C. announced that it was going to build a new electronically controlled switchyard in Elkhart, Indiana and shut down the Niles' facilities. Not only were many jobs lost when the new yard opened in 1958, but because of the new equipment, fewer men were required. The whole community suffered economic damage with the loss of the large payroll as well. There had been some previous reductions in the post-WWII years because of a general post-war reduction in railroad traffic. There were also manpower cuts that had come with the change over from steam to diesel locomotives since the maintenance and operation of the diesels was simpler

The loss of the Niles' yards though had made land and buildings available for other industrial uses. Much of the old yard and some of the buildings are in use today as an industrial park. The remaining terminal grounds are used extensively for recreation of various types.

This faded old photograph shows what appears to be a Civil War-era Great Moghul-type locomotive inside the old roundhouse C. 1870.

On Front Street (about where the Niles Fish Market is presently located) the Big Four built their depot buildings. On September 5, 1898 a large crowd gathered to meet one of the trains. The reason for the gathering is no longer sure, but local tradition has it that they gathered to see some notorious criminals who were being transported up from Indiana to face trial at the county seat. Bicycles were all the rage at that time. Can you count the number of them visible in this photo?

59

After 15 years of waiting for the "temporary" depot, the community was pleased and relieved when the new depot was built in 1890/91. The depot housed an elegant restaurant, offices and lodging for MCRR employees, as well as the passenger lounges, ticket offices, and baggage rooms.

The new depot was viewed with pride by both the community and the MCRR itself. The community saw it is a mark of tremendous civic progress, a symbol of all that was good, beautiful, and modern. The Railroad spent considerable money on, to quote the 1892, *Niles Daily Star,* "the palatial structure which now adorns the new depot grounds as a passenger house. Money and art have not been spared to make this building attractive. All of brownstone, plate and stained glass, and the most accomplished taste can do, is hear (sic) illustrated. The traveler when he rolls into this luxurious station, will be tempted to enquire further of the town which the great Michigan Central company has delighted to so adorn. The new building is typical of our progress." Fulsome as the editor's words were they were indeed accurate. The depot facilities brought much attention and renown to Niles. One of the town's major industries was the result of a chance stop by a man who was seeking a new location for his business.

MCRR Gardens

In 1893, the MCRR established a greenhouse and gardens in Niles on the depot grounds. The Columbian Exposition (the Chicago World's Fair) was to take place that year. The Niles' station was the last stop on the route that most visitors from the East Coast and overseas would make before their arrival in Chicago and the MCRR wanted to make a good impression.

The greenhouses were built and operated as was the MC Park (as the gardens were called) under the careful supervision of Mr. John Gipner, a German-born and trained master gardener. The 10,000 square feet of floor space located inside the glass greenhouse was used to grow a wide variety of flowers, tropical garden stock such as palms and exotic ferns, and other decorative plants for the railroad's use. The greenhouses also provided all of the cut flowers for daily use on the lines' dining cars (each table had fresh flowers on it) as well as flowers and plants for offices, restaurants, lounges, etc, in all of the lines' facilities.

In addition to designing and maintaining the ornately landscaped depot park and the greenhouses in Niles, Gipner and his crew landscaped other MCRR facilities across the country. However, it was the Niles' facilities which became famous for their floral beauty. For many years, every woman passenger who stopped in Niles received a small bouquet of fresh flowers. That little courtesy, the beautifully designed and meticulously maintained flower beds and ornamental plantings of the park, and the large greenhouses, earned Niles the title of the "Garden City;" not only along the MCRR route but across the country and around the world. According to an early newspaper account, "The travelers from foreign lands have carried home the lore of the railway's floral factory (as) one of the astonishing things one might find in America."

The MCRR greenhouses in Niles were the largest complex in a system of many all over the country. It served as the headquarters and was used as a model by all of the MCRR gardeners. This snapshot shows part of one of them.

In 1911 the National Railway Gardners' Association held their annual convention in Chicago. Their president, Mr. Patrick Foy, who was the head gardener for the Norfolk and Western Railroad (headquartered in Roanoke, Virginia) was quoted in a hometown newspaper in an article describing the convention, as follows:

"Over the Michigan Central, the delegates went to Niles, the headquarters of the gardening system of that (rail)road, where again a hearty reception awaited the visitors at the hands of the head gardner, Mr. John Gipner, and his assistant Mr. R. J. Rice. 'The Niles station is the most beautiful in Michigan if not in the United States' Mr. Foy said, 'and I was especially pleased with that portion of my trip.'"

A railroad worker poses for his picture in front of an elaborate floral bed on the depot grounds circa 1920. Niles was known to railroad travelers, not only for its gardens, but also for its history. The MCRR featured an advertisement, enticing passengers to "learn about Niles while you dine" which appeared on the back of their dining room menus.

Adjoining the depot was the MC Park where passengers met friends and family, waited between trains, or simply rested on its benches. A refreshing, enjoyable stroll could be had while admiring the beautiful gardens which were accented by artistically planned fish ponds.

A large flower bed east of the depot building which spelled out the name "NILES" in floral colors was a prominent feature of the depot park. Postcards showing this flower bed were popular souvenirs for many years.

George Forler posed with his sons who ran the grocery store after it was rebuilt and restocked.

This original frame boardinghouse and grocery store were destroyed by fire in 1889 but they were promptly rebuilt.

FORLER

Since the railroad depot area was some distance from the Main Street business district, a separate small business district developed in the area adjacent to the railroad. In 1865 Mr. George K. Forler opened a boardinghouse on the southwest corner of 5th and High (now Wayne) streets across the tracks from the depot. Soon a whole row of rooming houses, eating places and other shops stretched along the south side of the tracks for the convenience of travelers and railroad workers. Many of those buildings are still standing, and though changed in appearance some are still in use as restaurants and saloons.

Christmas Dinner at Forler's Restaurant. Menu

Consomme of Chicken with Noodles
Celery   Olives

Baked Brook Trout, Lemon Sauce
Hollandaise Potatoes

Ox Tongue, Sliced Lemon   Ham
Corned Beef

Chicken Salad   Escalloped Oysters

Roman Punch

Loin of Beef, Drip Gravy
Roast Lamb, French Peas
Turkey, Oyster Dressing, Cranberry Jelly
Illinois Prairie Chicken a la Paysonne
Mallard Duck, Currant Jelly

Lettuce   New Onions   Radishes

Mashed Potatoes   Sweet Potatoes
Sugar Corn   String Beans   Hot Slaw

Mince Pie   Pumpkin Pie   Lemon Pie
Christmas Plum Pudding, Wine Sauce
Tapioca and Apples, Cream Sauce
Black Fruit Cake   White Mountain Cake   Washington Cream Cake
Vanilla Ice Cream a la Meringue
Tea   Coffee   Milk

George Forler (in the hat) posed with family members and hotel employees for this picture in the lobby of the newly reopened hotel in 1890. The original building had burned the year before.

This is the way the block between 5th and 4th looked about 1900 after things were rebuilt. Additional restaurants and lodgings were added on the corners beyond both 5th and 4th streets in later years.

Postal card view showing MCRR locomotive terminal for repairs and maintenance of the rolling stock.

Several large steam powered excavators were used in the construction of the yards. Millions of cubic yards of dirt were moved by tip carts like these in the grading work the project demanded.

Many types of equipment were used to build the yards. Here a horse drawn grader is leveling the ground for the siding leading up to the synthetic ice plant.

In the 1930's, the locomotive shops in Niles helped build this experimental streamliner for the N.Y.C. it was called the *Bullet*.

The icehouses were an important adjunct to the railroads. The ice, either cut from the lake or made in the synthetic ice plant, was stored in these large buildings. The conveyers transported the ice to the appropriate level for storage.

The mass of ice stored in an icehouse was so well insulated with sawdust that when one of them burned to the ground only the outer layers of ice melted. Fire hoses were needed though to extinguish the burning building.

Large cakes of ice were skidded down the conveyers and into the railroad cars to keep the fruit and produce properly chilled.

Around 1890 High (now Wayne) Street was still unpaved, but it was the main route used by livery services to transfer passengers and baggage between the two depots.

The *Wolverine* eastbound out of Niles (depot tower and 5th Street viaduct visible in the background) about 1940.

In his unsuccessful re-election campaign President Jerry Ford campaigned by rail across his home state. Here he greets the crowd at the Niles Depot.

Even though the steam locomotives were extremely powerful, heavy loads and long trains sometimes required two locomotives pulling together to make it up the long grades out of Niles.

67

FASHIONS

Fashion has always told a story of a community and Niles is no exception. Sometimes society dictated the styles, while at other times economics determined one's wardrobe.

In a small town like Niles there were people of prominence and there were those who did without. At times a persons' wealth was made obvious by his or her attire. At other times it was not as visible. Where a wealthy woman might have an abundance of decorations and accessories displayed in a photo, another woman of more modest means might be seen wearing a very similar outfit. It could be difficult to discern between the two. The photos would not tell that one woman may have owned many such outfits and posed for photos on numerous occasions while the other, less prominent woman may have donned all of her finest "Sunday best" for a once in a lifetime photo session.

This pictorial fashion story begins in the mid-nineteenth century when photography became common. Pictures depicted faces void of smiles, dresses meant to slope the shoulders downward, and hair in a center part with long curls behind.

Ladies' fashions changed much more dramatically than men's fashions through the years. The reasons for this are virtually unknown ... though they have been argued over for centuries.

A reflection backwards over the changes and adaptations of colors, shawls, bustles, fans, parasols, and hats is a purely enjoyable experience.

Niles was a small town, and in times past, because of transportation and communication limitations, fashion trends were usually a slight bit behind the population centers of the East. Regardless of the fashions in another part of the country, one can be sure that it was at some point in time worn by the citizens of Niles.

C. 1860

C. 1860

Dark colors were worn by women over 40 years of age, while at the same time the introduction of aniline dyes made brilliant and sharp color combinations possible. Plain, flat trimmings based on stripes, classical, and military motifs reflect the influence of the Civil War on the world of fashion.

Wide hoops began to replace the numerous petticoats worn under skirts made from a wide choice of fabrics. These included wools, taffeta, silks, velvets, and satins.

C. 1860

Tightly laced, very small corsets achieved the desired tiny waist. If the ideal 17 inch waist was an absolute impossibility, every attempt was made to duplicate it as closely as possible. A gliding walk was adopted to help control the crinolines while perfect balance was also required.

C. 1860

Children were often dressed to mimic their parents as well as other adults. The war became a part of everyday life at home. The military look of this very young girl's apparrel was only surpassed by the exact copies of uniforms frequently made for children's wear. These costumes were accented by military toys such as drums, toy weapons, and toy soldiers.

C. 1870

The very latest in fashion in 1870 was the "new look" in ladies' hair. Centrally parted and pulled back to reveal the ears, the hair was arranged in a chignon or in long curls. For the first time in Victorian hair styles, the front hair is frizzed or prettily curled to form a fringe.

69

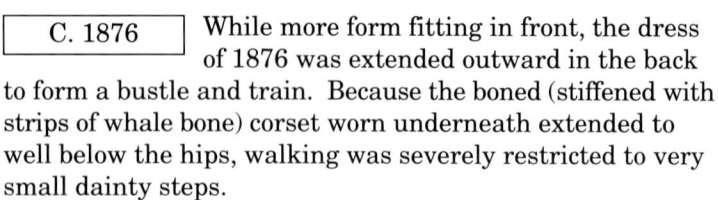

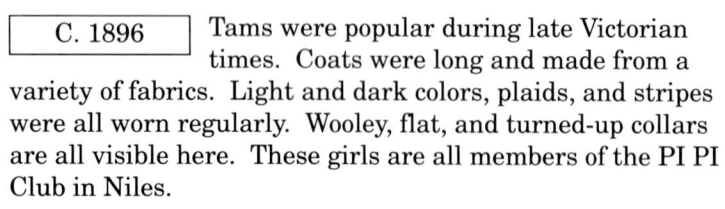

C. 1876 — While more form fitting in front, the dress of 1876 was extended outward in the back to form a bustle and train. Because the boned (stiffened with strips of whale bone) corset worn underneath extended to well below the hips, walking was severely restricted to very small dainty steps.

C. 1876 — Dresses in the 1870's consisted of a bodice and skirt with the bodice being lightly boned and usually having a high or V-shaped neckline. Elaborate decorations adorned the back of the train including flounces, fringes, braids, and bows. Hats were small and tipped forward, and were worn for informal occasions. Bonnets were reserved for more formal wear.

C. 1896 — Tams were popular during late Victorian times. Coats were long and made from a variety of fabrics. Light and dark colors, plaids, and stripes were all worn regularly. Wooley, flat, and turned-up collars are all visible here. These girls are all members of the PI PI Club in Niles.

C. 1885 — In 1885 the three piece lounge suits were popular among the men. A "true gentleman" may have preferred the more sophisticated look of a two piece suit with a white shirt and a striped tie worn underneath a "Covert" coat, which was short and often had a velvet collar. This was also the era of the drooping waxed moustache and the bowler hat. The expectation for gentlemen was that they be stiff, formal, and self-consciously dignified.

C. 1886 — When fur reached its peak in popularity, it appeared in capes, boas, and mantles. Hats became larger, taller, and more unusual.

C. 1885 — Skirts in the mid-1880's began appearing with gathers and pleats as is seen in the dress of this young girl. High buttoned boots or laced up shoes were the order of the day for the fashion conscious, including children. Hair was dressed neatly and close to the head. Even a small child was accessorized with fur trimmings such as those visible on the bodice cuffs.

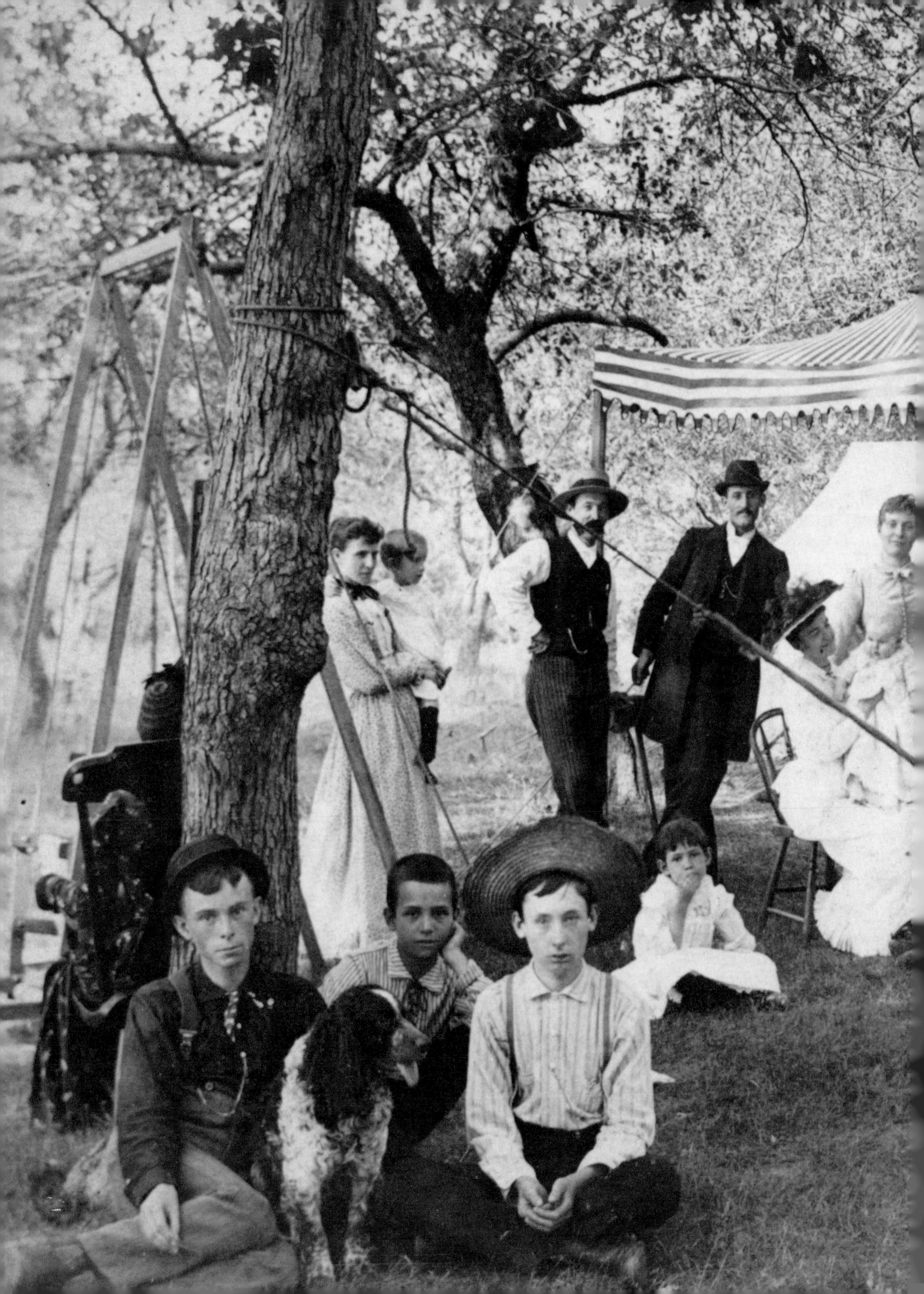

C. 1890 Even during a leisurely camping trip to Barron Lake, fashions were very important. Calicos, stripes, pleats, and suspenders can all be seen here, along with a wide assortment of hats.

A mid-Victorian bathing beauty poses to show off her bathing attire. Unlike the other dresses which varied from high to low waist, tight or loose; the waist of the bathing dress was formed by a simple belt. There was plenty of room for comfort and even the stockings were worn in the water. Hair was fashionably very long, below the waist and was carefully worn pinned up at all times other than when swimming. Summer swimming was a welcome relief since indoor bathing and hygiene were much different than now. Hair was to be washed once a month, thus avoiding the possibility of diseases caused by too frequent washings.

Hats around the 1900's were very large with upturned brims on one side and the brim on the opposite side turned down. Gathered chiffon, ranging in color from pastel shades to bright orange and dark brown accented the underneath as well as the top surfaces of the hats. Trimmings included tulle and lace, ribbons, cherries, nuts, fancy feathers, stuffed birds, and just about anything else that would stay put on the hat.

C. 1900 Around the turn of the century, skirts and blouses replaced dresses as the common attire. Belts were something new and varied from small to wider V-shaped ones that drooped in front to accent the waist. Blouses are "pouched" in front. Shoes were often excessively pointed with stockings of black, brown, or scarlet color.

Fine sewing and detailed embroidery were trademarks of a well-bred woman. If one was afforded the time, training, and the desire to complete and wear her own handiwork, it represented a certain amount of prosperity. Lockets and watches worn at the neck in this manner were a popular accessory for both men and women at the turn of the century.

After the turn of the century, "mannish" or tailor-made ensembles were still very popular. The coats were three-quarter length with narrow sleeves. The skirt is pleated and top stitched to below the hip level.

C. 1910 Travel wear meant a whole different set of clothing for men and women. A voyage confronted the traveler with weather changes as well as inconveniences within their living quarters, even for that era. Posed photos on the deck made for great entertainment for guests once one returned home. Because such adventure was rigorous and expensive they were limited to the experienced and the wealthy. Hats secured with long scarves were the best way to guard against the smoke, steam, and fog.

C. 1918   The silhouette was now straightened. Everything was loose fitting and comfortable to wear. Laced up shoes were worn with stockings of black for day wear and colors for evening. The influence of the "War to End All Wars" is clearly evident in this women's adaptation of a sailor's suit.

C. 1920   Around 1920, for those who dared, permission was granted to cut or "bob" one's hair. Shocking and controversial, it was one sure way to make your own personal fashion statement.

C. 1926   Dresses by 1926 were similar and uniform in cut. Skirts were visible from hip to knee and worn under long straight tops. Two piece costumes, jumper sets, and cardigan coats were popular. Long bead necklaces, drop earrings, and slave bracelets were common accessories. Hats had helmet-like crowns and narrow brims. Felt hats were also popular.

C. 1930   Dresses in the early thirties were pouched and slackly belted at the waist. Hemlines flare and dip at the sides. Low V-necklines with collars were sometimes filled in by an undervest of similar material. Hair is longer forming a roll in back. Brims of hats are of various sizes and dip down all around, or drooping over one eye.

C. 1934   Trousers for men are more tapered at the hems. Sports jackets were narrow in cut, tightly fitted with broad lapels. Pullovers, and plus-fours were popular for casual and country wear. Straw hats were still around promoting a sporty look for summer.

C. 1930   The thirties' styles for women's bathing suits might best be described as having simple basic lines. A scooped neck, long, one-piece suit (probably wool) was worn by both women and little girls. Gone were the undergarments, and long outer dress-like tops with pantaloons. Finally women had the freedom to truly enjoy a swim.

C. 1930   In the 1930's women's dresses shortened considerably from the previous decade. Specific lengths were becoming more of a discretionary issue. The long narrow pointed shoe was gradually replaced with a wider, flatter, french-heeled shoe. Notice the woman's hat and the man's interesting, patterned necktie.

C. 1940   "Resembling the miniature couple on the top of a wedding cake" best describes the neat, perky look of this couple. The lines on women's clothing were long and slimming. The late thirties and early forties were a more mature, elegant, and relaxed era in fashion. Ready made clothing flooded the market and was available to everyone. This altered the appearance and fit of clothing. With a small tuft of fabric accenting the simple hat, add a hand bag and suede gloves, and a simple dress or coat became elegant.

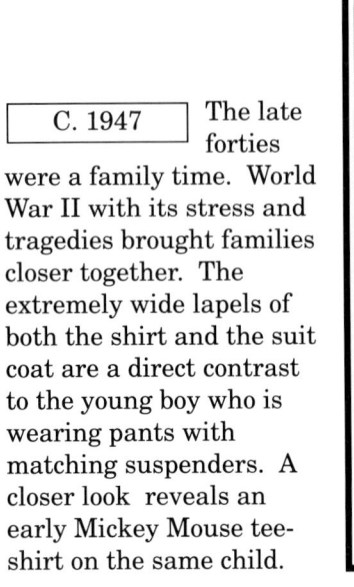

C. 1947   The late forties were a family time. World War II with its stress and tragedies brought families closer together. The extremely wide lapels of both the shirt and the suit coat are a direct contrast to the young boy who is wearing pants with matching suspenders. A closer look reveals an early Mickey Mouse tee-shirt on the same child.

C. 1940   With pretty curled hair framing the face; penny loafers, white anklets, and a leopard-look trimmed coat created a complete look for a young lady in the 1940's.

C. 1950   Stripes, florals, and polka dots were familiar patterns during the mid-1950's. Belts were simple and narrow, often made from the same fabric as the dress. Dresses were flared at the hemline with gathers or pleats at the waist. Short, curly, or "permed" hair was in style. Charm bracelets were a very popular and highly desired item. Note the charm bracelet on the lady second from the left. Men's single breasted suits were worn with either a bowtie or a conventional necktie. There are always those who prefer the style of their own generation, no matter what the fashions dictate.

C. 1950   During the mid-1950's, the very young girls wore dresses nearly all of the time. Even as families traveled, little girls were all dressed up as if to go to church. Fabrics were delicate and feminine making ironing a constant necessity. Sitting on a prickly wool chair in layers of gathered or stiffened tulle half-slips, little did these two sisters realize that the dawn of polyester ready-to-wear perma-press was soon approaching.

As easy care fabrics came into prominence in the fashion world, they ushered in a new era and a new concept of clothing. Not only did the fabric content change, but also the care of one's attire and one's purchasing habits were affected. Women's pantsuits gave women a sense of freedom, while at the same time the new outlying shopping centers gave all shoppers new territory. The social issues of the turbulent sixties made their statements with blue jeans, tie-dyed tee-shirts, long hair, and beards. As communities like Niles gradually adapted to the world around them, both the need and the desire for a central shopping area nearly vanished. Shops and their fashions in downtown Niles either gave way or learned to co-exist with the large, faceless, and impersonal shopping malls.

NILES DOWNTOWN

The earliest settlement of the village of Niles was on the flat land next to the river. Early development was centered in the area between the present day bridges. It was there that the first log houses, stores, inns, and taverns were built. The first half-century of downtown Niles history predates the invention of photography, and no sketches or drawings from that period are known to exist. The only graphic images available from that era are early land plat drawings and they fail to give an accurate impression. They often show proposed streets and lots where the original forest still stood. However, they do give an idea of the dreams and aspirations of those first settlers.

1868-1870. Hamilton's Store, second store from the southwest corner of 2nd and Main.

Taken about 1867, this shows the south side of Main from almost the corner of 2nd to the river. The trusses of the early bridge are barely visible at the foot of the street.

In 1869, the western half of the north side of Main between 2nd and 3rd looked like this. Note the "museum" sign on the third floor. Clem Barron opened his museum there in 1842. It was one of the earliest in the country. Some of his artifacts are still in the Fort Saint Joseph Museum in Niles.

Gradually, the log buildings were replaced with frame and clapboard structures, many built in the "Greek Revival" style then popular. In 1839 the first brick building, the Arcade building at the northwest corner of 2nd & Main, was built. Soon brick "fireproof" buildings began to replace the wooden structures. Fire was the biggest threat to the town in that era. By the time of the first photos in the 1860's, few of the original wooden buildings are visible because many had been burned and replaced with brick.

As the business district developed, commercial buildings were built farther and farther up the hill, until, by the turn of the century, very few residences still stood on Main Street between the river and 5th Street. Businesses also spread to the north and south of Main Street as well. In the early years the area north of Sycamore Street was low and swampy. Travelers headed north from Niles had to travel the road on the top of the hill (5th Street) until they were well north of town. Over the years that area was ditched, drained, and then filled and built up, particularly when the railroads came in in the late 1840's. It later became an area of industrialization, particularly along the river and Front Street.

Main Street looking west from Second Street at 9:30 a.m. on October 2, 1898. The arched iron truss bridge is clearly visible at the foot of the rutted muddy street.

Above: Looking uphill from the intersection of Second and Main streets.

81

MEDICAL HOSPITALS

Soon after the establishment of the City of Niles in 1829, medical services were available to its residents. The first doctor in the city was Dr. E. Winslow who came here in 1831. By 1850 there were at least half-a-dozen physicians to choose from in the community. Early medical care was based on the home care of the ill or injured, with the physicians coming to the patient. Centralized facilities for the care of the sick were uncommon although in the case of epidemic illness the victims would often be quarantined into one facility. This was done, not so much for the convenience of those caring for them as for the protection of the rest of the community. These facilities were known as "pest-houses," often an appropriate description.

During the Civil War, a private residence in Niles was used as a medical care facility for the men of the 12th Michigan Infantry unit, which was organized and trained here in the city. Such facilities were uncommon however, and home care remained common until the end of the century.

Toward the end of the nineteenth century some doctors began to open up private hospitals either in their own homes or in spacious houses they acquired for that purpose.

One of the earliest identified hospitals in Niles was the private hospital of Dr. William H. Smith at 109-111 South 2nd Street (this is where the BPW substation stands below the police/fire station). Dr. Smith had his offices and housed patients here until about 1910. A Dr. Carr continued to operate the facility until at least 1918.

PAWATING HOSPITAL

Niles had long needed and waited for a real hospital, and in 1921 a sub-committee of the Chamber of Commerce met to form the Niles Hospital Association. Their original plan was to incorporate and raise $50,000 to acquire a spacious house at 202 South Lincoln. However, four years passed with no action and when the organization finally took place, the option for the South Lincoln property had long expired. However, the mansion formerly occupied by the Dresden family was available. An option was taken and plans were made to convert the vacant mansion to a "modern hospital." The whole community joined forces to raise the funds required with fall festivals, style shows, and other fund raising events. However, such events fell far short of the funds required.

On Christmas eve of 1925, the *Niles Daily Star* announced in banner headlines that Mr and Mrs. F. J. Plym were going to give the citizens of Niles a hospital. The Plyms would spend $100,000 to purchase the Dresden estate (long known as Castle Rest), renovate it according to plans prepared by the Hospital Association's architect, and turn it over to the Association to operate. This marvelous Christmas gift would provide the town with their long awaited hospital. It would be up to the community however, to fund the furnishing and operating costs of the facility. The community's reaction was such that pledges for the expense of equiping all 11 of the private rooms and the wards were in hand by New Year's Day. The next year was spent in converting the old mansion. It opened its doors to patients in November of 1926   Major additions and renovations over the years gradually surrounded the original structure until in 1964 the remnants of Castle Rest were razed and replaced.

Castle Rest was originally built, right after the Civil War by G. A. Colby who owned several grain mills. He made large profits during the war supplying flour to the army. Part of these profits paid for the construction of the mansion. In the 1870's it passed into the hands of the Millard family who were involved in the development of Niles first industrial park around the dam on the river.

Castle Rest was later acquired by the Dresden family. It had been vacant for some time and had fallen into disrepair (and some disrepute). With repair and renovation, it once again became "a home of elegance and gracious living." It was occupied by the family until Mr. Dresden's death in 1924. It was sold by his surviving children to the Plyms for use as a hospital.

Standing on the west river bluff overlooking the Broadway Bridge and most of the downtown area, Castle Rest occupied a prominent position in the community as is shown in this early 1900 photo of the bridge.

83

For many years a wooden Indian graced the front of the south wing of the hospital. The kids in town (and more than a few adults) just "knew" that it was a statue of Chief Pa-Wa-Ting for whom the hospital was named. Growing up we learned that the name of the hospital, Pawating (with the accent on the "ting" for the really knowledgeable), was the Potawatomi word for the river crossing next to the hospital where the ancient Indian trade path, the Great Sauk Trail, forded the river.

As to the old statue, more mature eyes could see that it was a cigar store Indian. Reputedly it was acquired at the 1892 Columbian Exposition by the Dresdens as a lawn decoration. In later years it deteriorated badly, was repaired, deteriorated again, was disposed of to a collector, and at last report has retired in the South. He has been replaced by another "wooden Indian," this time a female who stands in the hospital lobby symbolizing Madeline Bertrand, the part Indian wife of the old fur trader, whose land grant included the land occupied by the hospital.

From the beginning one of the prominent features of the beautifully landscaped Castle Rest grounds was its elegant gazebo. As the hospital expanded, the gazebo was faced with demolition to make way for a new wing. It was "rescued" by the ladies of the Garden Club who had it moved to the grounds of the home on Chicago Road known as the Kimmel house after the Civil War officer who had it built. It still stands there as one of the two surviving relics of the original Castle Rest (the other is a marble mantelpiece displayed in the new hospital lobby). The gazebo shows clearly in this detail from a 1923 postcard view.

By 1956, the date of this photo, modern additions were beginning to engulf and replace the Castle Rest portion of the hospital. Within a few more years even this remaining facade was gone and only the marble fireplace in the new lobby and memories would remain of the old mansion.

In the last years of the nineteenth century, the mansion became the location of a notorious medical "diploma mill" known as St. Luke's Hospital. Set up and advertised as a hospital, its only real business was selling fake medical school diplomas by mail. They were sold to "quack" doctors to hang on their office walls. Elegantly printed diplomas on "Heavy Royal Linen Paper" were $5, "Imitation Parchment" was $7.50, and "Genuine Parchment" copies were $10. At least, it was said, the parchment was genuine. Though their business was pretty much a secret, word got out since a number of local high school students got jobs lettering up the bogus diplomas. Ironically, the operation, though a complete fraud, was perfectly legal under Michigan's laws of that time. The laws regarding medical school diplomas and certificates were changed as a result of this incident. The two con men who ran the operation were eventually run out of town by a combination of local physicians and the vengeful ex-wife of one of the men who tipped off some of their creditors. The "doctors" fled town promptly with their creditors in pursuit.

85

E.B. Ives was a popular and prolific portrait photographer in Niles around the turn of the century. Many of the portraits used in this book were made by him. The composite picture used at the front of this book showing many of Niles citizens was made by his assistant, Ruth Hulin, as a collage of some of the studio proofs.

Above: G.H. Jerome was a very prominent citizen of Niles in the last quarter of the last century. A lawyer, judge, and politician, he was active in Republican affairs during the Civil War. His large estate, Sabine Farm (the area just south of Silverbrook Street in present day Niles), was the site of his private fish hatchery, the first in the state. His interest in fishing led him to become active in the movement of fishermen for state regulation and protection of sport fishing. He was named to be the first state fish commissionser and is to be considered one of the founders of today's Department of Natural Resources.

Left: William Reddick was a local businessman who owned a wire goods' factory along the river just north of the Main Street bridge. He was also a very avid photographer. A large percentage of the C.1900 photos of downtown Niles in this volume were originally taken by him.

PERSONALITIES

Around 1880 a young girl arrived in Niles on one of the "orphan trains" and was adopted into the family of George Morris. Ella Morris attended Niles public schools but died of consumption shortly after graduating from high school. She will always be remembered as one of the "Orphan Train girls."

At the turn of the century Kate Noble had a chewing gum factory at the corner of 4th and Wayne streets. She supplied gum to accounts all over the mid-west, including the Wrigley

Ella Champion was one of the town's most-loved teachers. She grew up in Niles, attended the local schools as a child, and spent her whole career as a teacher in the Niles' school system. In the 1899 City Directory she is listed as a first grade teacher at Central School. She is also highly regarded as an artist whose hand-painted greeting cards are considered local treasures.

PARADES

Like the rest of the nation, Niles has always loved a parade. Early newspaper accounts describe the parades that were a vital part of political campaigns in the pre-radio and television era. Holidays, starting with the Fourth of July and in later years Memorial Day, were usually celebrated with a parade. Circus and Wild West shows used parades to advertise. Main Street has seen them all.

Everybody loves a parade and the circus parades drew large crowds as they passed through town on their way from the railroad depot to the fields on the west edge of town where they would set up. These elephants led the bandwagon and the rest of the parade on June 20, 1900.

The dedication of the Fort Saint Joseph boulder was the focus of the Fourth of July parade in 1913. One of the Boy Scout troops created this float as their entry in the parade.

The marching band followed by local dignitaries and a delegation of well groomed young ladies led this Decoration Day parade in 1914.

In the late 1920's or early 1930's, the Noble Shoe Store sponsored a Kiddies' Day Parade and a drawing with the little car as a prize. The lucky winner and his envious friends posed with Mr. Noble in the alley behind the store for this group photo.

In the days of horse-drawn vehilcles, parade participants marched down the hill. With the advent of the automobile, as viewed in this photo of World War II soldiers and sailors, participants paraded up the hill with ease.

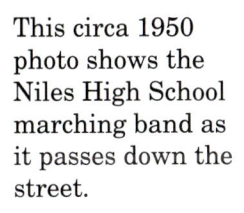

This circa 1950 photo shows the Niles High School marching band as it passes down the street.

91

EARLY SCHOOLS

The first school in Niles was the Carey Mission school, founded by Isaac McCoy in 1822. While its purpose was the education of the Indian children of the area, the children of the traders, Burnett and Bertrand, also attended. Their children had previously been sent to Detroit for their basic education. The curriculum at the Carey Mission School consisted of the basic "3-R's" (read'n, rit'n, and 'rithmetic) as well as domestic and agricultural arts.

When the Anglo-American settlers started to arrive in the late 1820's, education was not an immediate priority, but by 1830 a private school was opened by Titus B. Willard. His school was located in a double log house on the north side of the 200 block of Main Street. He lived and took in boarders in one half of the cabin, and held classes in the other half. By an Act of the Territorial Legislature in 1827, communities were required to "teach the children to read and write and instruct them in English or French languages, as well as in arithmetic, orthography (spelling), and decent behavior" for six months each year.

A one room clapboard building was built on the northeast corner of Third and Sycamore in 1833 for use as the community's first "common" or public school. As was usual in frontier towns, it was also used as a church until regular church buildings could be built.

Although basic education was just beginning in

The original Union School was built in 1855-56. It was three stories tall and situated on a four acre lot where Central School would later stand. It housed four departments; primary, junior, senior, and academic. There were eight teachers and 450 students the first year. Students came from as far away as Goshen and St. Joseph to attend in Niles. The original Union School was demolished in 1920 to make way for the Central School building.

A "report card" of 1860. Class standing was based on an average of attendance and deportment, in addition to scholastic achievement. The school year was divided into three terms.

Certificate of merit awarded to Mary Bond 1851-2. Note the use of religious sentiment. Early public education made liberal use of the Bible as a basis for ethical teaching and as a readily available text book.

Niles, institutions of higher education were started almost immediately. In February of 1836 an advertisement appeared in the Niles newspaper for the Niles Academy which would open in April to teach *"the usual branches of English education together with Mathematics and the Latin and Greek languages."* This was necessary because, as the ad continued *"it is well known to many of our citizens that several distinguished gentlemen at the east, who are desirous to adopt this place as the place of their future residence, are...unwilling to come....because there is no school in which their sons could receive...a liberal education."* The desire to attract prominent citizens from the East was a common feature of fledgling pioneer communities. At about this same time, two private schools were opened providing training in fine and cultural arts in addition to general education for young ladies.

In 1838 the University of Michigan opened a branch in Niles as part of a system of branch campuses at eight locations across the state. It was designed to prepare students for entering the University and to provide local training for elementary school teachers. Unfortunately, the national financial crisis of the late 1840's caused the branch system to be abandoned.

Early public education in Niles was rather haphazard because it depended on the ability and availability of the teachers, but by the 1850's the town had developed to the point where public pressure demanded better quality schools. As a result, several neighborhood school districts were merged and the first Union School was constructed in 1855-56.

The Niles community was very proud of its school and erected this fountain in the "park-like" school lawn as a symbol of its sense of accomplishment. The schoolgrounds were often used for civic functions and political rallies. In 1900 Presidential candidate William Jennings Bryan used them for one of his campaign speeches.

Niles High School was opened in 1912 on the same block as the Union School. Designed to provide for the high school students, it was soon also used for lower grades as well because of a significant increase in the number of students. By 1919 overcrowding had forced the school system to put 500 of the students on half-days. As a result, an additional school building was constructed which replaced the old Union School.

Above: Niles students posed for a class or school picture about 1880 at one of the neighborhood schools.
Below: For the nation's Centennial in 1876, photographs of schools across the country were sent to Philadelphia for display. This picture of the Niles High School students was posed for that purpose.

Harry Mansfield was both respected as a kind and patient teacher of children with special needs and feared as the Niles' School Truant Officer.

Mr. D. O. Woodruff was the president of the Niles' School Board for many years. He returned to Michigan from the Gold Rush in California in 1852 as a wealthy man. He purchased a large farm estate just west of the city on Chicago Road.

Mrs. E. J. Collins was a teacher in both the Catholic and the public schools at various times in the 1870's and 1880's.

Additional primary schools were needed and in 1864 three new brick schoolhouses were built. One of them was this Fourth Ward School (shown as it appeared in 1899) which housed the students of the former West Niles Primary Branch School which had been meeting since 1861 in rooms rented from St. Mary's Church.

The Ferry Street School opened in 1868 as the "colored school." The black students had attended classes in the old common school starting in 1865. However, the segregated schools were abolished by 1872 and the "colored school" was rented to the German Church. In 1875 it was back in use as a regular primary grade school.

The Niles Public School System, at its maximum enrollment in the late '60's and early '70's, had one high school, two junior highs, and five elementary schools in the city. During this period they had constructed two new nearly identical elementary schools, one on the north side and one on the south side. In addition a new elementary was built on the west side, and two identical Junior high's were constructed. The C. 1930 Eastside elementary continued to be used and the old Central school complex was used for elementary classes, administrative, and support functions.

As the peak of the "baby boom" passed however several of these schools were closed and various functions changed. The old Central School complex was demolished. At the present time only "Ring Lardner is still in use as a Junior High. The former Ballard Junior High is used as the elementary school for the west side of town. The former Westside elementary is used as the administration center and space is rented for continuing education from several colleges which offer local classes. The Southside school is used for special educational services and Northside is used as a school sponsored pre-school and day care facility.

East Side School

North Side School

West Side School

South Side School

Junior High

"Satisfaction Guaranteed or your money

Montgomery Ward

In 1872 Aaron Montgomery Ward, along with his brother-in-law partner, George Thorn, established the first mail order business in the world with the controversial motto "Satisfaction Guaranteed or Your Money Back."

Aaron Montgomery Ward was born in 1843 or 1844 (there is some confusion among historians about the actual year). He came to Niles as a boy at the age of seven or eight with his family and lived in a house at the corner of Sycamore and Front streets. He was the oldest son of the seven children of Sylvester Ward and Julia Anne (Greene) Ward. He attended Miss Brown's Select School until his mid-teen years (approximately age 14) when he quit to work, first in a local barrel factory and then in a brickyard. By age 17 he had left Niles for a better paying job in a shoe store in a little town north of Niles. He soon left that to become a sales representative for a general merchandise house. In the course of his sales travels he met his brother-in-law (and future partner) in Kalamazoo.

In 1866 Montgomery Ward moved to Chicago, the transportation hub of the nation. In 1872 he married Miss Elizabeth Cobb, the sister of George Thorn who became his business partner. In 1873 using a total capital of $2,400, including $800 from George, he started his mail order business. The establishment of the world's first mail order business had begun.

His motto of "satisfaction guaranteed" caused great concern on the part of his competitors who could not or would not stand behind their products. (Even his partner questioned his soundness of mind and business sense). In that mid-to-late Victorian era the general public perception of purchasing was strictly "let the buyer beware." In 1873 the *Chicago Tribune* published an article intending to expose the "questionable" firm of Montgomery Ward and their unheard of guarantee. Consequently, Ward sued them for libel

This is one of the very first Montgomery mail order catalogues. From the beginning Ward directed his sales promotions to the rural people and the farmers. That is why it was addressed to the "Grangers," a popular political and social organization of the farmers.

Aaron Montgomery Ward

back" "This is a pledge and on it I will build my business." *A. MONTGOMERY WARD*

and won! This resulted in a turn-around endorsement by the *Tribune*. A. Montgomery Ward continued this policy until his death on December 7, 1913, at the age of 69. The retail mail order business bearing his name still claims this policy to be in effect today.

Because of the growth and expansion of the Montgomery Ward mail order business, a new outreach to the customers was considered. Finally, after much deliberation, the first Montgomery Ward retail store was opened in Marysville, Kansas, in 1926.

During Ward's successful career, his parents and family continued to reside in Niles until their deaths. Sylvester A. Ward died in Niles in 1898, and Julia Anne (Greene) Ward died in 1908. Both are buried in the Silverbrook Cemetery. Montgomery Ward was a very private man who made many trips back to Niles to visit friends and family. He shunned all public attention during these visits, though he was later to provide financial security and housing for his parents.

The business was a success ever since the first one page catalogue was printed in 1872. The enterprise of Montgomery Ward and Company was destined to be a billion dollar success story by 1984, and it is still serving customers today.

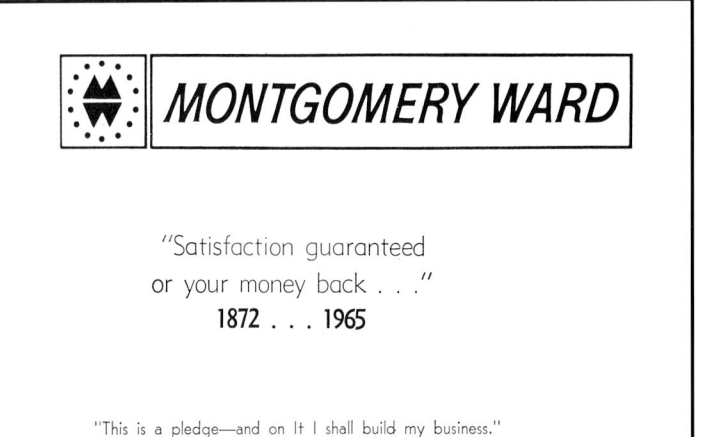

MONTGOMERY WARD

"Satisfaction guaranteed or your money back . . ."
1872 . . . 1965

"This is a pledge—and on it I shall build my business."
. . . A. MONTGOMERY WARD—1872

This ad from a 1965 high school yearbook is for the Montgomery Ward Niles retail store which first opened its doors to the public in 1938. It later expanded by adding a second floor, more buildings, a warehouse, drive-in auto repair and sales annex. It was closed, as were many other retail stores in small communities, by the corporation in the mid-1970's.

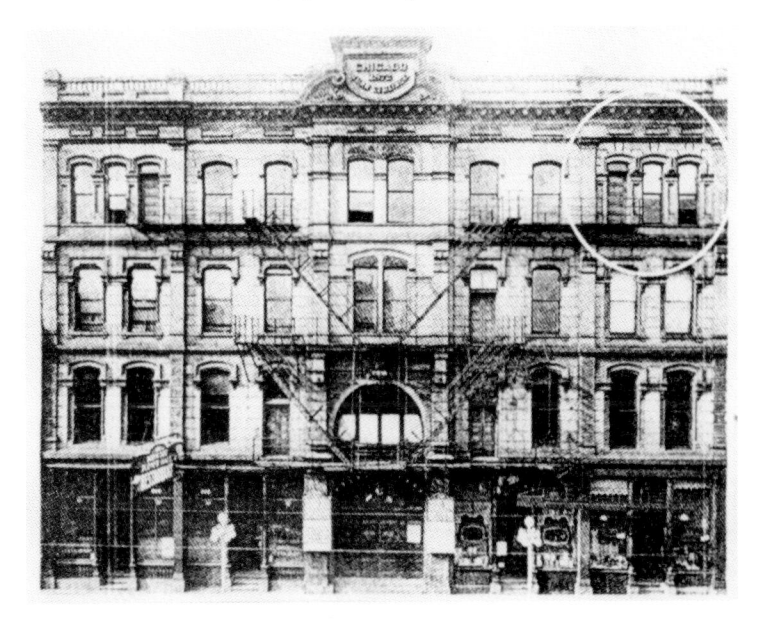

Circled is the rented Clark Street (Chicago, Illinois) offices where Montgomery Ward and Company had it's beginning.

Listed in 1899 as the nation's second tallest building; the building was visited earlier by thousands of tourists during the Chicago World's Fair (the Columbian Exposition). It was promoted at that time as the world's largest mercantile store. Ward was very active in efforts to beautify and preserve the scenic aspects of Chicago's lakefront. For these activities he was later to be called "the Watchdog of the Lakefront."

The first floor of the company's Wabash Avenue (Chicago, Illinois) warehouse, as it was portrayed in his 1881 catalogue.

This house, one of the "kit" houses available from Ward's mail order catalogue, was built by him for his mother about the turn of the century. It was located on North St. Joseph Street in Niles, it was razed in the early 1980's to make way for medical offices.

Montgomery Ward and his wife Elizabeth on the porch of his mother's home during one of their frequent visits back to Niles.

RING LARDNER

Ringgold Wilmer Lardner was born in Niles on March 6, 1885. The son of Henry Lardner and Lena Bogardus Phillips Lardner, he attended Trinity Episcopal Church where his maternal grandfather had been a minister many years before. Ring, as he was called, sang in the choir as a young boy and enjoyed playing the piano for pleasure and to entertain guests for most of his life.

His early schooling came from private tutors in the family home on Bond Street. Later he attended the Niles public schools and graduated from Niles High School in 1901 at the age of 16.

Ring's first job out of high school was with the local gas company. His first boss, Bascom Parker, the owner of the company, was quoted in a 1938 issue of the *Niles Daily Star* as saying that Ring was "too soft hearted for the job." His hidden talents were soon to be noticed.

Often he would go to the local ball games and write down his personal comments on them. There are varying accounts of just how his writings came to the attention of the area newspapers. He accepted, with great uncertainty, a job with the *South Bend Tribune,* and it is said that Mr. Parker held his job open at the gas company in case the newspaper job didn't work out.

He later moved to Chicago, where from 1907 to 1910 he worked for the *Inter-Ocean, Chicago Examiner* and the *Chicago Tribune* newspapers as a baseball writer.

In 1911, Ring Lardner married Miss Ella Abbot of Goshen, Indiana, at her parent's home. At this point in his career he was finally beginning to see the fruits of his labors in the journalistic field.

In the early years his journalistic experience was devoted extensively to sports. He traveled with the Chicago baseball teams covering the games and wiring back detailed reports for the daily paper. In his years associating with and writing about the Cubs and the White Sox, both on and off the field, he became an expert on the game and its personalities. From this experience he based the play *Elmer the Great,* which was later made into a movie. He also developed the fictional character "Jack Keefe," an illiterate baseball player who told of his big league experiences in letters sent home to his friend "Al." Ring included these humorous accounts in his sports column. They were later incorporated into the book *You Know Me, Al* which was published in 1916.

In addition to covering baseball and many other sports, he was given the assignment of writing the daily column "In The Wake Of The News" for the *Chicago Tribune* as a result of public response to his entertaining writing style. While he was not the very first writer of a daily column, he is credited by literary historians with being the one who "created the daily column." At one point he started publishing articles in his Monday column, which were purported to be written by one of his sons. Written in a comical childlike manner, they were based on the antics of his own children. They were later compiled and published as *Bib Ballads*.

In 1919 he resigned from the *Chicago Tribune* and

Ring with family and friends. He is posed holding a baseball bat; he had a lifelong fascination with the sport.

This sketch of Ring is based on a picture of him working at his typewriter. It is by local artist and illustrator, William Blackmun.

devoted himself entirely to literary work while continuing as a nationally syndicated columnist. His columns were published in New York, St. Louis, Boston and many other cities all over the country. The full power of Lardner as a creative writer of short stories flowered during this second phase of his career. It was during this period he wrote the classics, *The Champion* and *Haircut* (which was based on an incident in a Niles barber shop).

Following the success of *You Know Me, Al*, he went on to write a series of books including *Gullibles Travels, The Big Town, How To Write Short Stories,* and others. In some of these works, Lardner utilized an American folk-type, the "wise boob" whose uncultured, wisecracking, ironic comments poke satirical fun at the illusions and pretentions of those around him.

By 1920 Ring Lardner was one of America's highest paid writers. His focus in writing broadened to include *The Love Nest, Anniversary,* and *Golden*

A caricature of Ring from the program of the Lardner Centennial Symposium held at Albion College in Albion, Michigan in March of 1985.

An early photo of Ring with his dog.

One of Lardner's many books which were known for their spontaneity, wit, humor, and use of American vernacular language, *Symptoms of Being 35,* was published in 1921.

This nationally syndicated comic strip based on Lardner's *You Know Me, Al* sports stories is from a 1923 *Niles Daily Star* newspaper..

Honeymoon, covering topics of wealth, power, and anger. Continuing the use of his wonderful gift for recording the way America speaks; he was also to write *Some Like 'em Cold* and *I Can't Breathe,* portraying the tensions of modern marriage.

Eventually, Ring moved to Great Neck, Long Island, where he resided for a number of years. Later he moved to East Hampton, New York, though he never forgot, or stopped writing about the scenes and people of his youth in Niles. After suffering for the last ten years of his life with tuberculosis, he succumbed to death at the early age of 48 on September 25, 1933, from complications of that disease and heart failure.

"His writings are a mine of authentic Americana, his service to etymology (the study of words and speech) incomparable" wrote H.L. Mencken in 1921.

One of Niles' "favorite sons," Ringgold Wilmer Lardner will remain an American literary hero.

The Lardner house still stands at 519 Bond Street. It was originally built by banker Rodney Paine and subsequently acquired by Henry Lardner in 1882. This classic steamboat Gothic style Victorian home has subsequently lost its sweeping verandah-style porches.

In March of 1985 Ring's son, Ring Jr. (who was one of the characters in *Bib Ballads* and *Gullibles Travels*) and other family members returned to Niles to see the family home and to visit the church the family had attended. They were in the area to attend the Centennial Symposium in honor of their father and grandfather. Left to right: Jim Lardner (Ring's grandson and look-alike), Natalie Lardner (Jim's wife), Tom Traverse pointing out the conversion of the family home to apartments, Ring Lardner, Jr. (center—and a well known literary figure in his own right) Mrs. Ring Lardner, Jr. (in hat) and Katy Lardner (with back to camera), not shown is Susan Lardner who was also part of the visiting family group.

Though trucks and automobiles were starting to appear, a number of different kinds of animals could be seen working on the streets of Niles during the early years of this century.

In this mid-winter scene a shipment of Reddicks Famous Mole Traps are being shipped on a horse drawn bobsled from the Reddick Wire Goods factory on the river at the foot of Sycamore Street.

Right: In 1902 the Youngs posed with their milk wagon, along with riding horses, carriage horses, and oxen.

Below: Leavett Brown is shown here in a 1907 photo with a donkey drawn delivery cart from the Niles Creamery.

104

Right: While we often associate the use of teams of draft oxen with an earlier period of our history, they were not unknown on the city streets as this circa 1890 photo shows.

An early auto magazine featured these caricatures of the well known brothers, John and Horace Dodge of Niles.

DODGE BROTHERS

John and Horace Dodge, founders of the Dodge Automobile Company, were born and raised in Niles. They were the sons of Maria Duval Casto and Daniel Rugg Dodge. They attended the Niles' public schools where they had excellent attendance records. Their older sister, Della (born 1863), graduated with honors. John Francis (born 1864) graduated in 1882. Horace (born 1868) dropped out of school a few months before graduation. Apparently the long hours spent in the machine shop with their father affected his schoolwork.

Their father, Daniel, was previously married to a local woman who bore him two children, Laura (1856), and later Charles Francis, who was born shortly before their mother's death.

Like many successful businessmen, John and Horace Dodge had a tendency to relish in a "rags to riches" tale of their past. While this legend has never been truly substantiated, both townspeople and the Dodge brothers "remembered" barefoot activities. However, it should be noted that going barefoot during most of the year for everyday activities was not at all uncommon for working class children. This was particularly true through the second half of the 19th century in small towns and cities like Niles.

It is evident that all was not destitute in the Dodge household on the north edge of Niles. Not only were the boys cleaned up (especially for church on Sunday), but as youths they were regular participants in Sunday School picnics, outings, and social activities in the community. Many of these occasions cost money which John and Horace seemed to have. In addition, the very early business of fence repair (including hiring three young boys) brought the brothers addtional spending money.

As the brothers grew up, they spent long hours in their father's machine shop. They eventually ran the business end during their high school years. The eager ambition of the boys prompted a family move a few years after they finished high school. A new location was sought which would be suitable for establishing a new business specializing in marine engines. After trying Battle Creek and Port Huron, they decided on Detroit ending a busy year (1886) of moving and traveling. In the 1880's foundries and machine industries were the fourth most important business of that city, even in those pre-auto industry years.

After separate jobs in different places of employment (involving typesetting machines and bicycle makers), they were eventually to reunite in business in 1887 when they joined a partner named Evans to found the Evans & Dodge Bicycle Company.

By 1901, John and Horace were already auto enthusiasts who had founded the Dodge Brothers Company and were on their way to a relatively rapid success story.

Raising to international fame and immense wealth as a result of the growth of the automobile manufacturing business, they were eventually to own mansions in Grosse Pointe, Michigan and Palm Beach, Florida, and castles in Europe. They entertained some of the wealthiest and most powerful people in the world, including European royalty.

During the years of their business and financial climb, the Dodges never forgot Niles. Returning in both 1915 and 1917 for sentimental reasons, they visited their parents graves in Silverbrook Cemetery. Family papers and photo albums depicting life in Niles are an important part of the Dodge family today.

John and Horace sitting in the back seat of the first car to roll off their production line in 1914.

106

The Dodge brothers made several different attempts to make benevolent contributions to the city of their youth. In 1917, an attempt was made to donate $50,000 for the establishment of a city park as a memorial to their parents. For various reasons the city officials rejected their gift.

After the Michigan Central Railroad moved its maintenance facilities and yards to Niles, the brothers put half a million dollars in the Reliable Home Building and Loan Association. The purpose of this investment was to help finance housing for the hundreds of families who were moved to Niles by the railroad. It financed the construction of the homes in the Eastlake Terrace Addition of Niles.

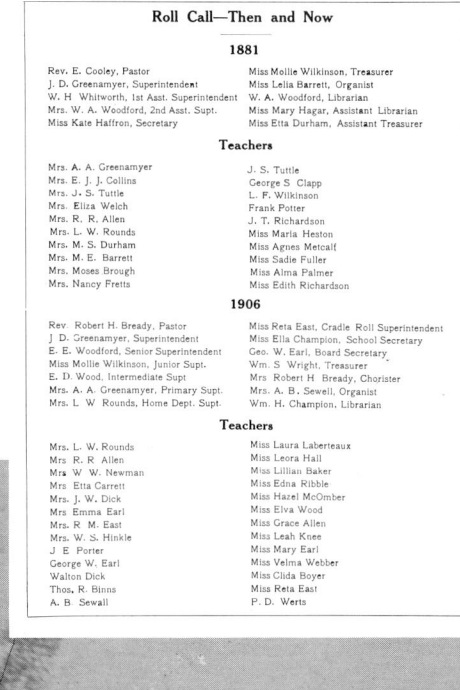

Roll sheet of the M.E. Church

Roll Call—Then and Now	
1881	
Rev. E. Cooley, Pastor	Miss Mollie Wilkinson, Treasurer
J. D. Greenamyer, Superintendent	Miss Lelia Barrett, Organist
W. H. Whitworth, 1st Asst. Superintendent	W. A. Woodford, Librarian
Mrs. W. A. Woodford, 2nd Asst. Supt.	Miss Mary Hagar, Assistant Librarian
Miss Kate Haffron, Secretary	Miss Etta Durham, Assistant Treasurer
Teachers	
Mrs. A. A. Greenamyer	J. S. Tuttle
Mrs. E. J. J. Collins	George S. Clapp
Mrs. J. S. Tuttle	L. F. Wilkinson
Mrs. Eliza Welch	Frank Potter
Mrs. R. R. Allen	J. T. Richardson
Mrs. L. W. Rounds	Miss Maria Heston
Mrs. M. S. Durham	Miss Agnes Metcalf
Mrs. M. E. Barrett	Miss Sadie Fuller
Mrs. Moses Brough	Miss Alma Palmer
Mrs. Nancy Fretts	Miss Edith Richardson
1906	
Rev. Robert H. Bready, Pastor	Miss Reta East, Cradle Roll Superintendent
J D. Greenamyer, Superintendent	Miss Ella Champion, School Secretary
E. E. Woodford, Senior Superintendent	Geo. W. Earl, Board Secretary
Miss Mollie Wilkinson, Junior Supt.	Wm. S Wright, Treasurer
E. D. Wood, Intermediate Supt	Mrs Robert H Bready, Chorister
Mrs. A. A. Greenamyer, Primary Supt.	Mrs. A. B. Sewell, Organist
Mrs. L W Rounds, Home Dept. Supt.	Wm. H. Champion, Librarian
Teachers	
Mrs. L. W. Rounds	Miss Laura Laberteaux
Mrs. R. R. Allen	Miss Leora Hall
Mrs W W. Newman	Miss Lillian Baker
Mrs. Etta Carrett	Miss Edna Ribble
Mrs. J. W. Dick	Miss Hazel McOmber
Mrs Emma Earl	Miss Elva Wood
Mrs. R. M. East	Miss Grace Allen
Mrs. W. S. Hinkle	Miss Leah Knee
J E Porter	Miss Mary Earl
George W. Earl	Miss Velma Webber
Walton Dick	Miss Clida Boyer
Thos. R. Binns	Miss Reta East
A. B. Sewall	P. D. Werts

Joseph Tuttle, a prominent businessman in Niles, was the superintendent of the Sunday School at the Niles Methodist Episcopal Church. He was also the young men's Sunday school teacher for many years and had been John and Horace's teacher. In 1919 John learned that Mr. Tuttle was about to lose his fine house because of financial reversals. This house, which stood on the corner of Main and 5th streets, had been the scene of many Sunday School gatherings in which the Dodges participated. Upon hearing that Tuttle was about to lose his home, John Dodge made arrangements and conferred upon Mr. Tuttle a life lease on the home.

Dr. F. N. Bonine

Frederick Nathaniel Bonine was born in 1863 in Niles in what was known as the Loban Harter house on the corner of 4th and Ferry streets. His father, Dr. Evan J. Bonine, was serving as a medical officer in the Civil War. Starting out as an enlisted private, he was appointed regimental surgeon for the Michigan 2nd regiment, and subsequently to the post of Surgeon-in-Chief of the Third Division of the 9th Army Corps where he was responsible for the care of 30,000 soldiers. Fred's mother, Evelyn Beall Bonine, was living with her sister, Mrs. Loban Harter.

F. N. Bonine graduated from the Niles public school system, and in 1886 graduated from the University of Michigan Medical School. That same year he married Viva Thomas, the daughter of Martha Finley Thomas. He then began his medical career as an eye-ear-nose-and-throat doctor in the second floor of his father's office at 126 East Main Street.

Dr. Bonine's work as an eye specialist eventually made him famous in the field of medicine. He treated over 50,000 patients a year, and once set a record by treating 517 in one day. His normal number of patients was about 200 a day. He also developed a non-surgical inexpensive treatment that cured cataracts. He was controversial among his professional peers, some of whom disliked the masses of patients, fast treatment and "cure-

GOLDEN ANNIVERSARY
FREDERICK NATHANIEL BONINE
M. D., LL. D.
Eye Specialist—Humanitarian—Sportsman
Citizen—Neighbor—Friend

Honoring His Completion of Half a Century Practice in His Native Niles
Four Flags Hotel   Febuary 25, 1937

Over 200 of the town's citizens turned out to honor Dr. Bonine at a special banquet in celebration of 50 years of service to the community in 1937.

Bonine Eye Clinic Bus Service
BETWEEN
CHICAGO, ILL. and NILES, MICH.

Safety
Comfort
Convenience

Modern Reclining Chairs
Well Heated
Radio

Bus leaves from ALL AMERICAN BUS STATIONS, 174 North State Street 9:00 A. M. - - - 514 South Wabash Avenue at 9:05 A. M., Chicago Time.

Above: Dr Bonine's patients came from all over the country. The trains regularly ran "Bonine Special" cars, from both Detroit and Chicago to Niles, as well as from other states, for the use of patients with vision problems. A Chicago bus company promoted a regularly scheduled bus, with stops in several Chicago locations, Gary, Hammond, and Michigan City to pick up and drop off patients. There were several boardinghouses in town which specialized in providing accommodations to his patients who needed to stay for repeated treatments.

Left: In 1916 this group lined up in front of the doorway leading up to the office and treatment room. Dr. Bonine is standing in the entryway in his shirtsleeves. Numerous accounts tell of patients lined up on the sidewalk, down the street and around the corner, waiting to get in.

all" reputation he had achieved. The controversy that resulted gained him further publicity, including a cover and feature article in a 1937 *Cosmopolitan* magazine. In spite of the work load and the publicity, Dr. Bonine was highly regarded as a community leader, serving for four terms as mayor. He was said to have often rendered his professional services free of charge to many local folk who could not afford them. He, like many of that generation, was a collector of Indian artifacts, curiosities, and souvenirs of his many travels. Many of these items were eventually presented to the local museum.

Dr. Bonine was also a highly accomplished athlete. In his youth, he set several world records as a runner, including one in 1885 for running the 110 yard dash in 10.4 seconds, a record which stood for many years. He maintained a life long fondness for all types of sports, especially professional boxing, baseball, and horse racing. Seldom, if ever, would he miss being ringside for a championship boxing match. He was a personal friend and physician to many of the boxing greats of that era, including Jack Dempsey and Joe Louis, and was a member of both the Boxing Commission and the Horseracing Commission for the State of Michigan.

In his honor, all city flags were flown at half-mast for 30 days after his death in 1941 at the age of 78.

Dr. Bonine was especially fond of the sport of boxing. He is said never to have missed a title fight from the days of the Corbett/Sullivan match until his final illness. He was able to name many prominent boxers among his friends and patients. He is shown in this news clipping with Jack Dempsey during the 1930's.

500 PATIENTS IN ONE DAY!

Read REX BEACH'S Amazing Story of Famous Eye Specialist

DR. FREDERICK N. BONINE
OF NILES, MICHIGAN

BENEFACTOR OF THE BLIND!
MIRACLE MAN OF MEDICINE!

Cosmopolitan

In its October 1937 issue, *Cosmopolitan* magazine had a feature article about Dr. Bonine. The popular author, Rex Beach, was assigned to write an "expose" of the "famous quack" but after spending several days in Niles observing and interviewing patients, the article that resulted not only exonerated Bonine, it was almost an endorsement. This advertising poster was circulated nationally by the magazine to promote sales of the issue.

Once one got up the stairs and into the office, the line continued around the walls and up to the examining chair. Dr. Bonine was an eclectic collector of "curiosities" and his office walls displayed many of his acquisitions in a most Victorian manner, as one can see in this 1925 photograph. If one was able to see at all, the wait was hardly boring.

Garden City Fan Co.

Garden City Fan Company is another major industry that was brought to Niles through the efforts of Carmi Smith and the Niles Businessmen's Association. They had started in Chicago in 1879, but accepted a relocation offer and came to Niles in 1900 to occupy a new factory on Wayne Street next to the railroad tracks where they made industrial fans and blowers. In the latter part of the century they moved into new manufacturing facilities in the airport industrial park.

Kawneer

Francis J. Plym

Born in Sweden in 1869 and brought to this country as a two year old, Francis Plym was greatly affected by a visit to the 1893 Chicago World's Fair as a young adult. He was amazed by the "world of the future," as it was illustrated through the machinery and blueprints on display. He had been a farm worker, which he disliked, and later had become a cabinetmaker and had been working in shops in several different mid-western states.

Influenced by his stepmother's perseverance and perfectionism, he enrolled at Northern Indiana Normal College for a term and from there succeeded in earning entrance to the University of Illinois School of Architecture. He finished there in three years, and then became a draftsman for an architect in Minnesota.

While changing trains in Nebraska on his way back home for a visit, he spotted an advertisement for a design competition for a library building, and decided to enter it. The competition, though unsuccessful, resulted in his meeting an elderly architect who took an immediate liking to him. The older architect allowed Plym the use of his office and equipment which subsequently resulted in a partnership between the two men.

Mr. Plym settled in Lincoln, Nebraska where he became very involved in the community. It was there he married Jane Barber in 1903. The new Mr. and Mrs. F. J Plym soon moved to Kansas City, where things were more up-to-date, because they believed that it would offer more opportunities.

By 1906 Plym was appointed to the office of city architect of Kansas City. In this position he became intimately familiar with the materials of modern commercial construction; copper, brick, concrete, steel, and glass. It was here he conceived an idea for making a metal frame for window glass that would support large panes of glass, have the right flexibility, and be erosion resistant. This made large plate glass storefront windows possible for the first time. Commercial window frames had always been made of wood, which restricted their size and caused design and maintenance problems. His innovative design ultimately changed the face of commercial architecture in America.

Plym was granted a patent on his concept in 1906. His product line was named "Kawneer," in reference to his first operations in a little sheet metal fabricating shop located near the Kansas River, which was known locally as the "Kaw."

He soon realized the need to be nearer to the East where his major market would be, so he went in search of a new location for his business. Stopping in Niles in 1906 while changing trains, he met a local businessman, Carmi. B. Smith, who was a prominent leader and promoter of the business community. Soon convinced by the persuasive Smith of the tremendous value of Niles' location as a transportation hub, (and further convinced by the offer of additional local business inventives) Plym decided to start his manufacturing plant in Niles at once.

Plym achieved success, not only locally but on a national level as well. He became one of the foremost authorities in the country on the design of roller machines for manufacturing formed metal, and on the heat treating of metals for roller shaping. As his business developed, additional plants were built in California and in Canada. In the early years, Plym had diversified his product lines, but in 1945 a corporate decision was made to concentrate on large volume in the Kawneer line of architectural and related products.

By their peak years in 1955, Kawneer had four main areas; architectural products, aircraft, appliances, and mill products, located in eight factories in the U.S. and Canada.

Over the years Kawneer Products developed into one of the major employers in the Niles area and contributed much to the community. However, in the 1960's and '70's, they were absorbed into one of the major metal industry conglomerates which gradually phased out all of the Niles operations. Production was shifted to other more profitable locations and the Niles plants were closed. The administrative offices were relocated as well. The Niles facilities were donated to the city and are being used by the local economic development foundation as a center for developing new businesses.

F. J. Plym and his Kawneer Company were Niles' first major industrial employer, but their contributions to the community have left an indelible mark.

The first Kawneer factory in Niles about 1907.

SIMPLICITY PATTERN CO.

Simplicity Pattern Company of New York moved their pattern printing and warehouse facility to Niles in 1927. They were able to take advantage of the skilled craftsmen of the area who had generations of experience in the papermaking and printing trades in local factories. At its peak in the 1960's and '70's, when they were producing more patterns than anyone else in the world, it was the largest employer in Niles with over 1500 workers. Many women were employed in the art department and as "folders," folding the various parts of the clothing patterns and stuffing them into envelopes.

At the Simplicity plant in Niles, workers trace master pattern markings on transparent glassine sheets.

Seventeen tons of light, sturdy tissue paper are made daily of pulp, scrap paper, and chemicals in the plant's own paper mills.

By hand, girls pick component pieces of the pattern and fold them into the rectangle size of the pattern envelope in four quick movements.

From this, their first factory building, National Standard has expanded to 17 facilities world wide. Their product list has expanded as well, from simple wire and twisted cable to specialty alloy products for the transportation, robotics, communications, health care, energy, agriculture, textiles, recreation, and food processing industries.

The present Niles facilities house the International Corporate Headquarters, a research and development laboratory, the Specialty Products and Welding Products plants as well as a major warehouse.

NATIONAL STANDARD

The National Cable and Manufacturing Company was started by William Harrah and Charles Anderson in 1907. In 1913 they acquired the Cook Standard Tool Company and merged them to form the National Standard Company. They began operations in Niles in rented facilities on the second floor of the Garden City Fan building.

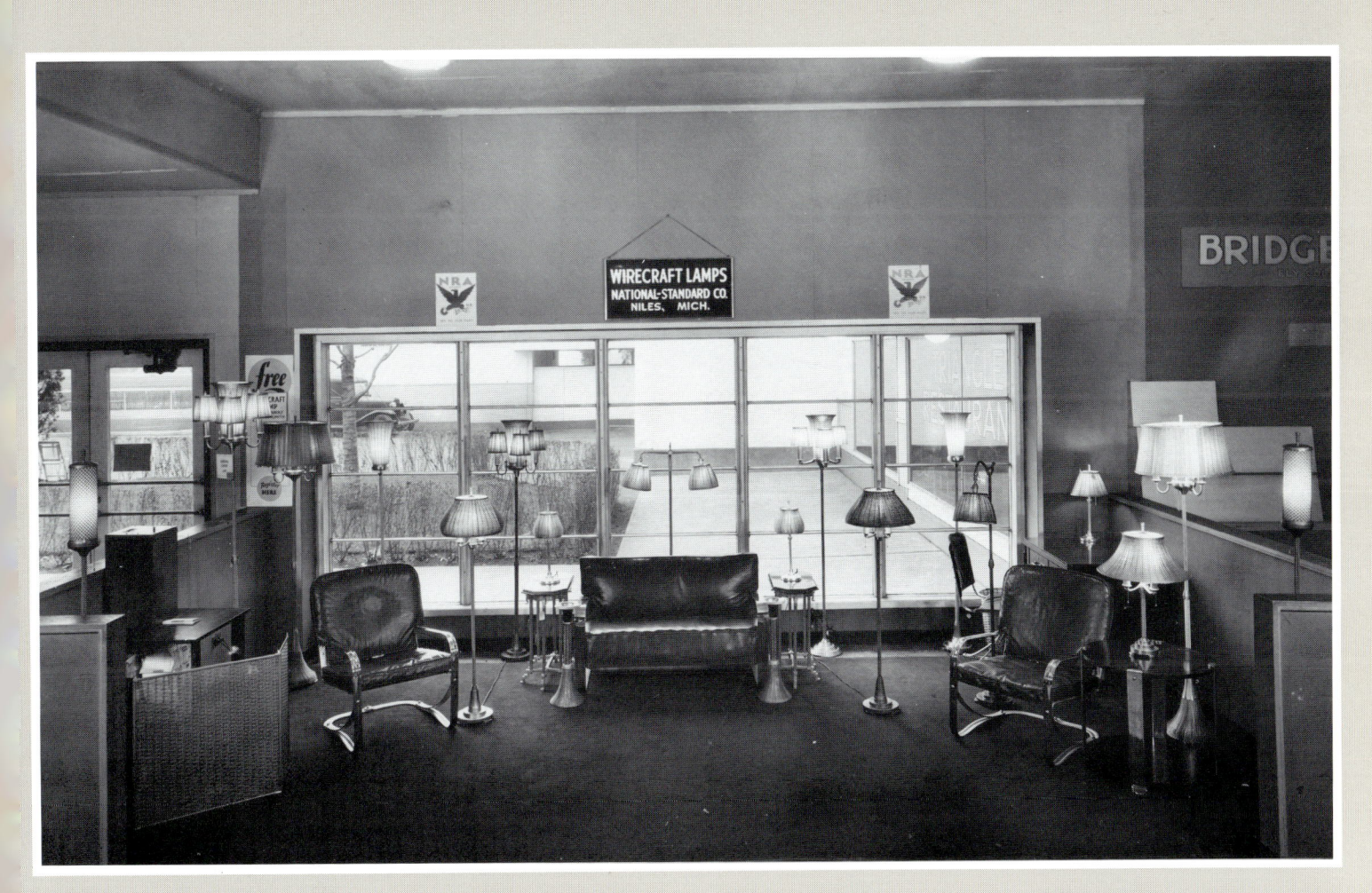

Most of National Standard's products were made for industrial use. However, they have ventured, on occasion, into unusual applications of wire technology. In the late 1920's and early 1930's they produced a unique line of Art-Deco inspired lamps, tables, baskets and other decorative items made of woven wire. Some of these items, particularly the floral baskets and floor lamps, were marketed to the funeral home industry. It was a short-lived effort and proved to be unprofitable. Now, however, the surviving pieces are commanding high prices among collectors. This photo shows part of the Wirecraft product line as displayed at the Century of Progress exposition in Chicago in 1933. The two chairs and the settee in the picture are now in the city's museum as are examples of many of the other Wirecraft items.

Recreation and Leisure Activity

Niles has always had a reputation for being a good place to relax. Very early on, people were coming here to "get away from it all." This was made possible and even promoted by the railroad which made easy transportation from the larger cities possible. The surrounding lakes, river, woods and fields encouraged outdoor recreation of all sorts. For generations, hunting, fishing, boating, and swimming, as well as more formal activities, have helped local people and visitors relax and unwind. Indeed, with the general change in industrial orientation, tourism and leisure-time activity bids well to be the major economic development of the future.

Even in 1936, there was a need to get away from the "modern" conveniences!

Whether it was Sunday or just a lovely evening, a buggy ride made it a "special" day.

F. C. Schmidt and his prized catch.

One lone woman poses with these triumphant fishermen.

In 1898, a woman fished in her everyday attire ... straw hat and all.

These men in 1894 almost made hunting look serious. Note the duck draped over the bow.

The diving tower at Kennedy Resort on Barron Lake was a popular place to show off and cool off during the summer heat.

Many local folk owned cool summer retreats on spring fed Barron Lake. This 1891 photo is of the French Cottage.

In addition to owning cottages many visitors came to rent at the various resorts. These two postcards are advertisements of the facilities at one of the resorts.

Island Park in the river was also a popular spot. Here a group of local citizens have gathered for the photographer. Back row: E.C. Griffin, Judge Coolidge, Mrs. Coolidge, Mrs. Griffin (Jennie Woodruff), Front row: Mrs. Newton (Louise Woodruff), Jerome, Orril Coolidge, Claudine Coolidge, Jeanne Griffin, Mrs. Otto W. Haisley (Harriet Griffin).

Baseball of course was always a popular sport in Niles, though these early teams lacked the uniforms and equipment of today's teams. This group was probably one of the early semi-pro teams to be found in Niles.

A local group of hunting buddies "clown" around.

Not only could you sit beside your car, but also on its running board.

A couple quietly fishes in one of the many area lakes.

Who hasn't just sat around with your favorite pet? Here Aleta Styers sits with her dog.

Aleta Styers enjoying the ultimate leisure time activity of many.

A proud hunter has bagged a big buck.

Golfing has enjoyed popularity in Niles at courses such as Plym Park and Orchard Hills.

119

Bridges

Bridges have been critical to the city's development since the river bisects the community. Bridges to replace the fords and crude ferryboats were among the first "improvements" planned by the early settlers. The first wooden bridges were rather crude but serviceable, often failing in the next flood or spring "ice out." The first bridge was here at the foot of the Broadway hill on the site of the old Sauk Trail Ford (the "pa-wa-ting"). It was built in 1836, but was rebuilt several times before this circa 1890 photograph. (Note the house on the left, it is the Smith/Carr Hospital house, and was to become the police station). This wooden bridge was replaced with a steel version about 1900, and then by the existing Cliff Eden concrete bridge in 1947.

Main Street bridge in August of 1900. According to the photographer's notes, everyone was on their way to the fairground east of town to see Pawnee Bill's Wild West Show. This graceful iron span was destined to last only 18 more years. It was built in 1868 and was not designed to handle the loads of "modern" traffic. It replaced an earlier wooden structure. It was itself replaced with today's concrete bridge.

The third bridge in Niles (other than the railroad trestle bridge) over the river was the "French foot-bridge." It was built in 1881 by the French Paper Mill and the city for the convenience of their workers who lived on the East side. It was originally a wider vehicular bridge, in the horse and buggy era. It was moved slightly downstream after a few years to accommodate the expansion of the mill. In later years it began to deteriorate, not being designed for motorized traffic, and by 1930 had become dangerous. After much discussion about its fate it was decided that the bridge would be narrowed rather than being demolished, and rebuilt as a footbridge. It survived as such until 1979 when it was closed by city order. It was again in dangerous condition and funds were lacking to repair it. There was considerable controversy within the community about its future until Mother Nature intervened and it was washed out in a major spring flood.

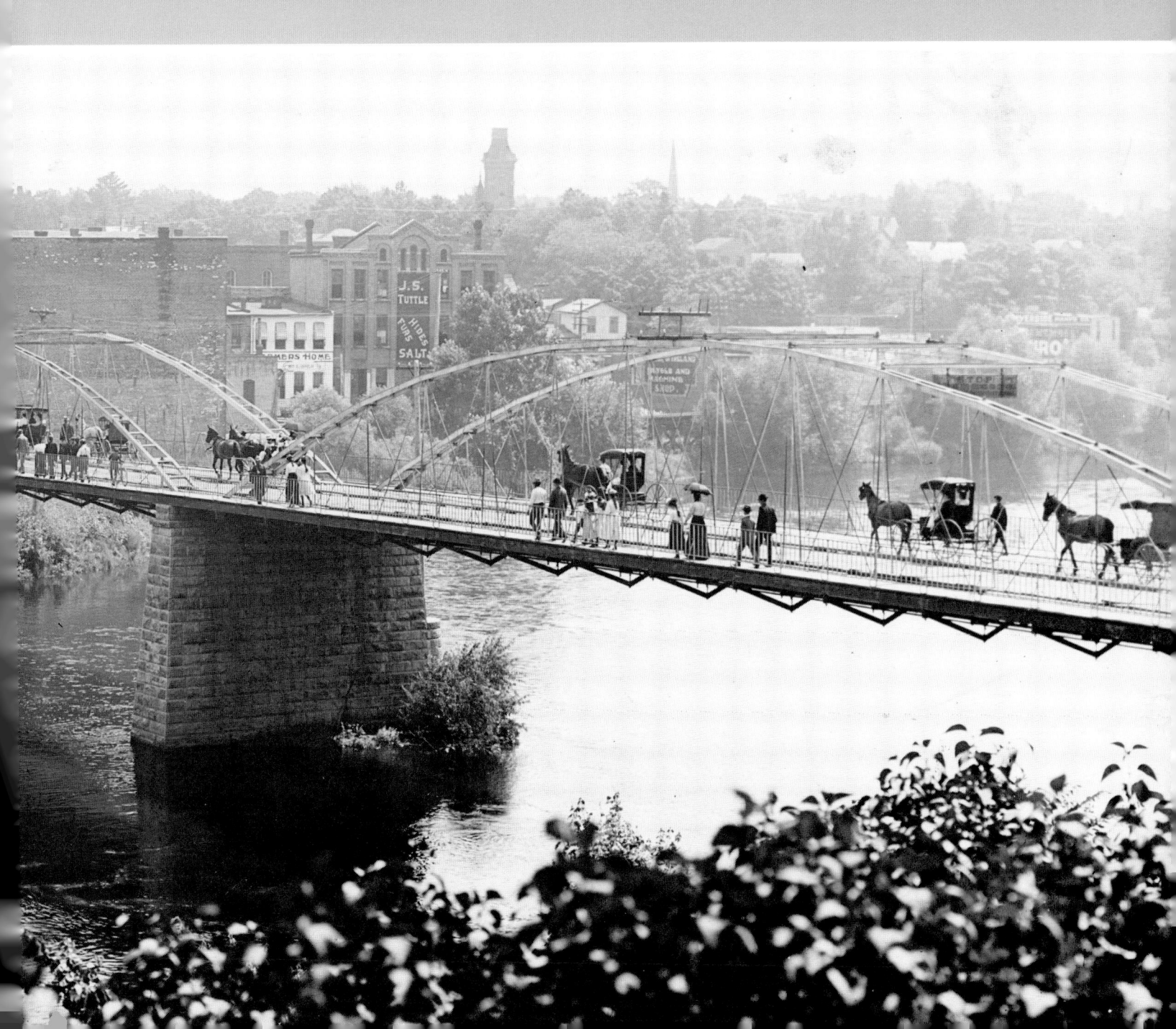

DOWNTOWN IN LATER YEARS

With the beginning of a new century the face of downtown Niles began to show changes which are readily seen in the various photographs in this book.

As the city entered the modern era the gaslights were first supplemented by, then replaced with, electric lights. In some of the earlier photos the carbon arc lamps can be seen suspended over the intersections, a few years later the carbon arc lamps are to be found on ornate lampposts along the street, then they were replaced with elegant multi-lamped round-globed incandescent streetlights.

At about the same time the dirt street which dated back to the days of the Indian's great Sauk Trail with its mud, ruts, and vegetable and animal residue was paved with bricks. The open running gutters were converted to subgrade sewers and the plank sidewalks were paved.

When the electric interurban railway was built in 1903, its main track ran down Main Street from 5th to 2nd street where it turned north again. In some photos though, a spur track can be seen running on west from 2nd to Front street and around the corner onto Front. Niles was well on its way into the twentieth century.

In this typical view from the bridge at the foot of the hill the Interurban track can be seen, as can quite a few early autos, the more "modern" street lights, and only a few horses. While undated this photo is probably from the very late teens or early twenties, based on vehicle styles.

In this earlier photo which probably comes from around the time of World War I or earlier the lines for the carbon arc lights can be seen. Horses and wagons are as common as autos and the Interurban spur line can be seen clearly in the brick paving.

This view of the north side of Main from 2nd to 3rd gives a good idea of how downtown Niles looked during the World War II era. Another newer style of streetlight can also be seen.

By the late '40's and early '50's the Main Street was beginning to look the way many of us remember it. The bricks are covered with asphalt. (The old bricks were dangerously slippery for modern traffic—especially when wet or icey.) The Kawneer store fronts are starting to be seen, particularly on the truncated remnants of the old Michigan Inn.

123

Architecture in Niles

Niles' houses have been built in many shapes, sizes, and styles in the course of the past three centuries; from the bark and reed-covered wigwams of the native Americans and the log houses of the colonial and pioneer eras, to the hi-tech, energy efficient, electronic, houses of the late 20th century. All have one thing in common, they have been "home" to the people of Niles.

Log houses provided shelter for the first century and-a-half of our history. They were the simplest, most easily built, and therefore the most common houses until sawmills made cut lumber available in the early 1830's. Early pioneers eagerly anticipated moving from log cabins into "real houses" as a sign of improved economic status and advancing "civilization." However, with the Centennial in 1876, log cabins were revived in the nostalgia for the pioneer era. That fascination is yet unabated as is shown by this National Park Lodge-style home built in 1943 on the west side of town.

Gothic Revival was the next type to be seen in Niles. This style was popular for both houses and for churches. It is easily recognized by the steeply sloped roofs, often with ornamental "gingerbread" trim along the eaves. Many show the orientation to "verticality" with a tall steeply pitched gable centered on the front of the house as this C. 1860 Niles home illustrates.

Italianate Style is used to describe those types derived from the domestic architecture of medieval Italy. It is characterized by informal massing of vertical elements such as towers, bays, and porches. These were combined with brackets at the eaves, key stones, arched windows, paired columns, etc. to create a unique and easily recognized look. Many of these elements are visible in the 1871 Henry C. Platt house which stood on the northeast corner of 4th and Sycamore until 1925.

The next "natural" or recognizable style to make its appearance in Niles was the "Greek Revival." Not only was it a clear architectural style, it also expressed a political and emotional affiliation with ancient Greece and democracy. It was used in both residential and commercial buildings and was built in many degrees of elaborateness. This house, owned by the pioneer Lacey family, is fairly typical with its triangular framed gable (the gable and roof pitch are the common characteristic of this style) and a simple four column portico. Many "Greeks" still survive in Niles in both common (or vernacular) and high ornamental style. Though introduced in the 1830's it was a very popular style which was used for new houses until almost the end of the century.

This centennial farm house, (the only one in Niles documented to have been owned by the same family for over 100 years) is of the vernacular style though it has some Greek Revival elements. It is almost entirely original to its 1859 date of construction.

Queen Anne was a style which was originally developed by an English architect in the 1870's. It became popular after the Centennial Exposition of 1876 in Philadelphia. This style usually shows a large irregular plan, a variety of surface materials, bay windows, towers, large porches etc. as this house on Broadway illustrates. Many Queen Anne homes were built as social statements by newly wealthy iron, timber, and industrial barons of the post Civil War "gilded age."

A more compact, and often more elegant and refined version of the Queen Anne is known as a "Princess Anne." A good example is the Richardson/Parkin house on Main Street. It is shown here in its modified form as the BPW building after being covered with aluminum siding.

Around the turn of the century a new form became popular for family housing. The Bungalow (of English Colonial Indian origin, as is the original house style) was popular all over the country and many local variations developed. Usually they were low, 1 or 1 1/2 story, homes with wide gable ends, exposed rafter ends which were often braced or bracketed, and with open porches. This California type bungalow on Regent Street shows a columned pergola (arbor) on each side of a central pedimented entryway replacing the more typical full-width porch. It is just one of the numerous varieties of the Bungalow home to be found in Niles.

Frank Lloyd Wright and his design team were the leaders in architecture around the turn of the century. They developed a style of home that characterized the American Mid-West. It came to be known as the "prairie-style." This house on Oak Street was strongly influenced by Wright's design. It shows the horizontal design, cross-axial spacing of the plan with extended wings, and great attention to the use of natural material and harmony with the environment.

Romantic Revival is the general stylistic term used for a wide variety of house types, which share a common feeling. Design and detail may be fashioned after a European cottage, (as in the almost Gothic-gabled Regent Street house), a castle, a chateau, or other picturesque, romantically inspired types (like the Main Street Dutch revival type shown below).

Above: The post World War II period saw a sudden and dramatic need for affordable housing for the large numbers of returning veterans and the ensuing "baby boom." Stimulated by the availability of construction funds and low interest loans to veterans, a whole new style of mass-produced affordable housing was developed. "Developers" planned, built, and sold whole neighborhoods of houses to this market. This Oak Manor house (c.1947) is typical of that basic type.

The concept of "planned development" soon spread into many parts of the city. Larger and more elaborate types of homes evolved as the economy recovered and the "baby boom" exploded. Soon the older core of the town was surrounded by developments, as old farmhouses which once were rural homes were engulfed by the city. As times have changed, the styles have gone full circle. Now replicas of earlier types and pseudo-Victorian houses are popular. Log houses are still being built, though now as "kit" houses. At the same time, the restoration of older traditional homes is becoming more common locally.

Whatever the architecture, the house served as a backdrop for the many plays of life. More than dramatic are the cold, stiff faces of this family properly posed during the Victorian era.

Chapter IV

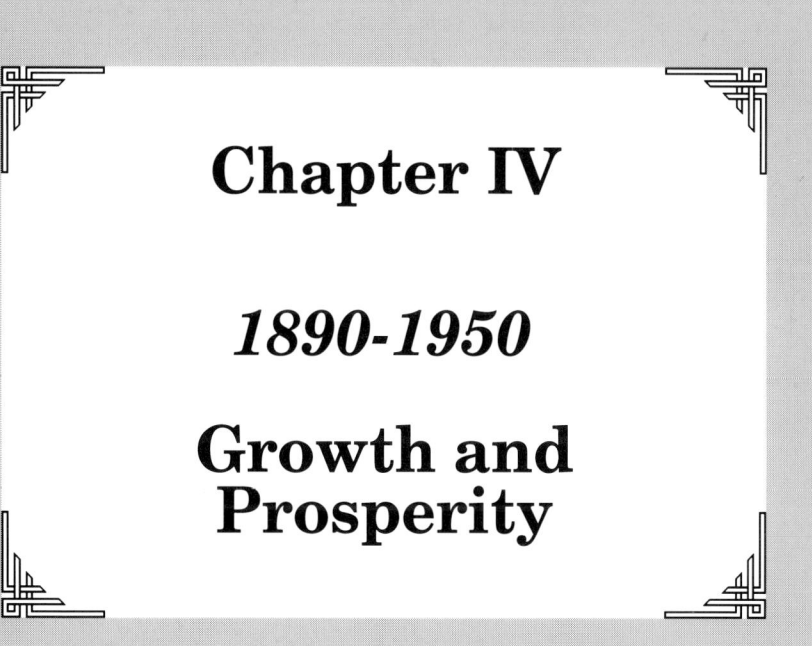

1890-1950

Growth and Prosperity

The years between the 1890's and the 1950's were an era of continued growth and relative prosperity for Niles. Continued industrial development provided an increasing economic base for the community. Existing manufacturing plants expanded and a group of local businessmen assiduously courted new companies in an effort to bring them to Niles by offering assistance and incentives for them to relocate. As a result of this activity, many more new industrial jobs were created in Niles during the early years of the 20th century. Local efforts were also successful in persuading the Michigan Central Railroad to relocate its shops and yards in Niles, thus adding another 1500 jobs. As a result, a community developed that was labeled as "the most industrialized, on a per-capita basis, town in America."

Increased jobs meant increased population, which in turn caused a need for newer and larger schools, health services, more stores and shops, all of the things a community needs to meet its needs.

Though individuals in the city may have experienced some difficulty during the World Wars and the "Depression," these events had a relatively minor impact on the overall economy. Almost all of the local industry weathered the "Depression" and actually improved their conditions during the wars, (World War II in particular).

Niles also saw a growing population during these years as people came from more depressed parts of the country looking for, and finding, jobs here. The growth of the population in this era caused changes in the social and political life of the community as the newcomers were integrated into the population.

There were other changes as well. The growth of the labor union movement had a definite impact as workers joined forces to obtain higher wages and changes in working conditions. Unionization was not always a peaceful process, since it was usually resisted by those who owned the businesses. While the unions succeeded in improving the workers lot, at times this tended to drive up the cost of operating the factories, (which had later negative effects) and altered the social and political fabric of the community.

There was also a change in the management of the businesses themselves. As capital was needed to expand and grow, the owner-operated companies were often forced to issue stock and take in new investors. Control over the companies gradually shifted from the founders, (who had strong ties and a sense of obligation to the community), to professional managers whose primary responsibility and loyalty was to the shareholders.

The invention of the automobile also produced a major impact on the lifestyle of the people of Niles. The "freedom of the road" replaced the iron bands of the trains. People could go where and when they wanted. New opportunities were opened in terms of employment and recreation. The landscape changed to accommodate the auto; streets and roads were improved and expanded, "sub-urban" housing became practical, and blacksmith shops and carriage houses gave way to gas stations and garages. As people started using autos more and more, passenger trains and interurbans were used less and less. With declining passenger revenues, the rail lines started cutting services and quality, which accelerated the process. By the end of the era, rail passenger service was almost at an end and the automobile age was in full swing.

HOTELS

Niles has long had a reputation for hospitality to visitors. The first hotel/tavern was built in 1830 and served as a social center for the whole community. It was also the muster point for the local militia and the county courthouse in the earliest years. More lodging facilities were eventually built to accommodate the flow of immigrants headed west. When the railroads arrived, hotel keeping became a significant trade in the town. In those early years the names of the hotels changed too often to make an accurate record possible, but by the mid 19th century Niles had at least half a dozen hotels. Because of the railroad traffic, newer, larger, and more modern hotels gradually replaced the older ones.

The northwest corner of Front and Main streets had been the site of some sort of hotel since the early 1830's. First it was the location of "old Diggin's," one of the first of the pioneer hostelries, then the Reading House (c. 1868), later called the Fanstock Hotel, then the Clifton House. During its heyday as one of the finest hotels in the state it was known as the Michigan Inn. As time and changing economics took over, it became known as the Miller Hotel. It lost its upper floors to a fire in the first part of the 20th century and eventually ceased use as a hotel. It was demolished during the early 1980's.

131

Hotels

Left: The last of the old wooden hotels, the Galt House, also known earlier as the Bond House, was destroyed in a spectacular fire in 1899. At the time it was built in 1881, it had been considered the largest hotel in western Michigan.

This is a December 1897 view of north 2nd Street. The two story porch and balcony of the Bond/Galt House Hotel is clearly recognizable on the northeast corner of 2nd and Sycamore. The old Central Hotel ($1.00 per day) stands adjacent to the alley on the west side of the street.

In 1867 this brick hotel was built on the southeast corner of Main and 4th streets. Known as the Pike House after its owner, Horace Pike. In this c. 1912 view the Pike house shows two wing additions, one along Main Street and the other along 4th. At this time Main Street, east of 4th, was a fashionable residential area with large homes. In the early 1920's it was razed to make room for a new hotel.

Four Flags Hotel

In the early years of this century during the time when Niles was an industrial "boom town," a group of prominent business and industrial leaders determined that the town needed a first-class hotel. This probably was not coincidental with the fire and subsequent decline of the Michigan Inn. A company was formed for this purpose in 1924 and stock was sold locally to finance the project. Within one year a quarter of a million dollars was raised, the site of the old Pike House acquired and construction begun. The new Four Flags Hotel "Niles new modern, fireproof hotel" opened its 78 guest rooms for the first time over the Fourth of July weekend in 1926. Until motels began to replace traditional hotels in the 1950's and '60's, the Four Flags Hotel was the city's premier lodging facility.

INTERURBAN

Berrien County has had communication problems over the years because of its shape and the distribution of its major centers of activity. Benton Harbor/St. Joseph, founded in the 1830's at the mouth of the river, and Niles in the southeast corner, were the major population and business centers. They were located at nearly opposite ends and corners of the county. Communications between the two were difficult and time consuming. This caused business and political problems, so it was with great anticipation in 1903 that citizens of the county awaited the opening of the Southern Michigan Railway, or the "interurban" as it was more commonly called. These light electrically powered railroads provided connections between cities on the same basis that the "trolley" lines did within them. In fact, some interurbans were extensions of the intra-city lines.

The Southern Michigan Railway and its Indiana branch, the Northern Indiana Railway, linked South Bend with St. Joseph. This 35 mile route had 65 regular stops, and a trip from end to end took about an hour and a half. Service was scheduled on an hourly basis. A round trip ticket cost $1.30. The cost for shorter trips averaged out to about two cents a mile.

Though started in 1901, construction was difficult and service from Niles to South Bend did not start until 1902. It was 1906 before one could travel the full distance. The interurban had a tremendous impact on the economy of the area. One of the first effects was the dramatic lowering of fares on the regular steam rail line which ran a parallel route. Ten round trips daily were run and a baggage and light freight service was soon offered. At either end one could connect with other interurban systems which allowed one to travel all over the mid-west. It was very popular with

The Interurban on Main Street during its first year of operation. Main Street was paved with bricks in September of 1902, so this picture must date from that first season of limited operation.

The construction crew laying track and grading on north 2nd Street south of Wayne Street.

This postcard view of the Niles triple-decker viaduct was famous and popular. It is reputed to have been included in an early "Believe it or not" column. It was located just south of the city limits where it was easily visible from the highway to South Bend. The upper level was for the Interurban track and the lower two were for regular railroad tracks.

tourists who used it to reach the beaches and the popular resorts. It was also used extensively to commute to work or for shopping. Property values went up along the route, particularly near the rural stops, since one could live "in the country" and work in town.

By 1910 the Interurban was having difficulties — complaints were voiced in the local papers about the quality of service. Most of the problems were caused by overcrowding — it was just too popular. The demand for constant service made it difficult to pull the cars out of service for maintenance.

In 1915 the southern counties of the state voted for prohibition well in advance of the national law prohibiting alcoholic beverages. This caused an additional increase in ridership of men heading south to Indiana to wet their whistles—and an increase of complaints about their conduct on the return trip.

During the war years private, unlicensed busses, often referred to as "jitneys," cut into ridership severely. That factor, when combined with the rapid post-war increase in automobile ownership, doomed the Interurban. Cost cutting measures did little to help them and made improvements in the quality of service impossible. In 1934 the line was shut down. Over the years since then many have expressed the thought that even today the old Interurban would be a real asset if it was still in operation.

The Interurban crews posed for this group photo.

In addition to passanger service the Interurban baggage and freight service along its route.

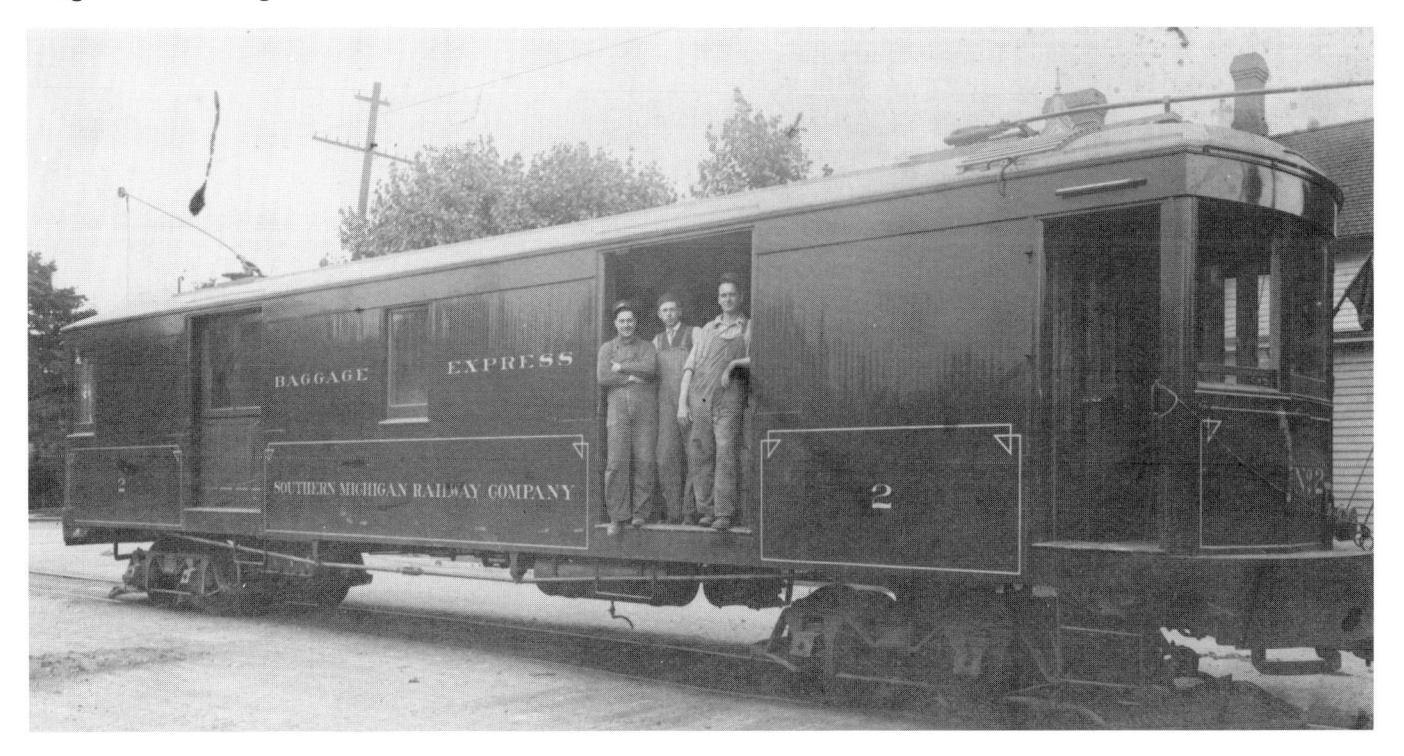

135

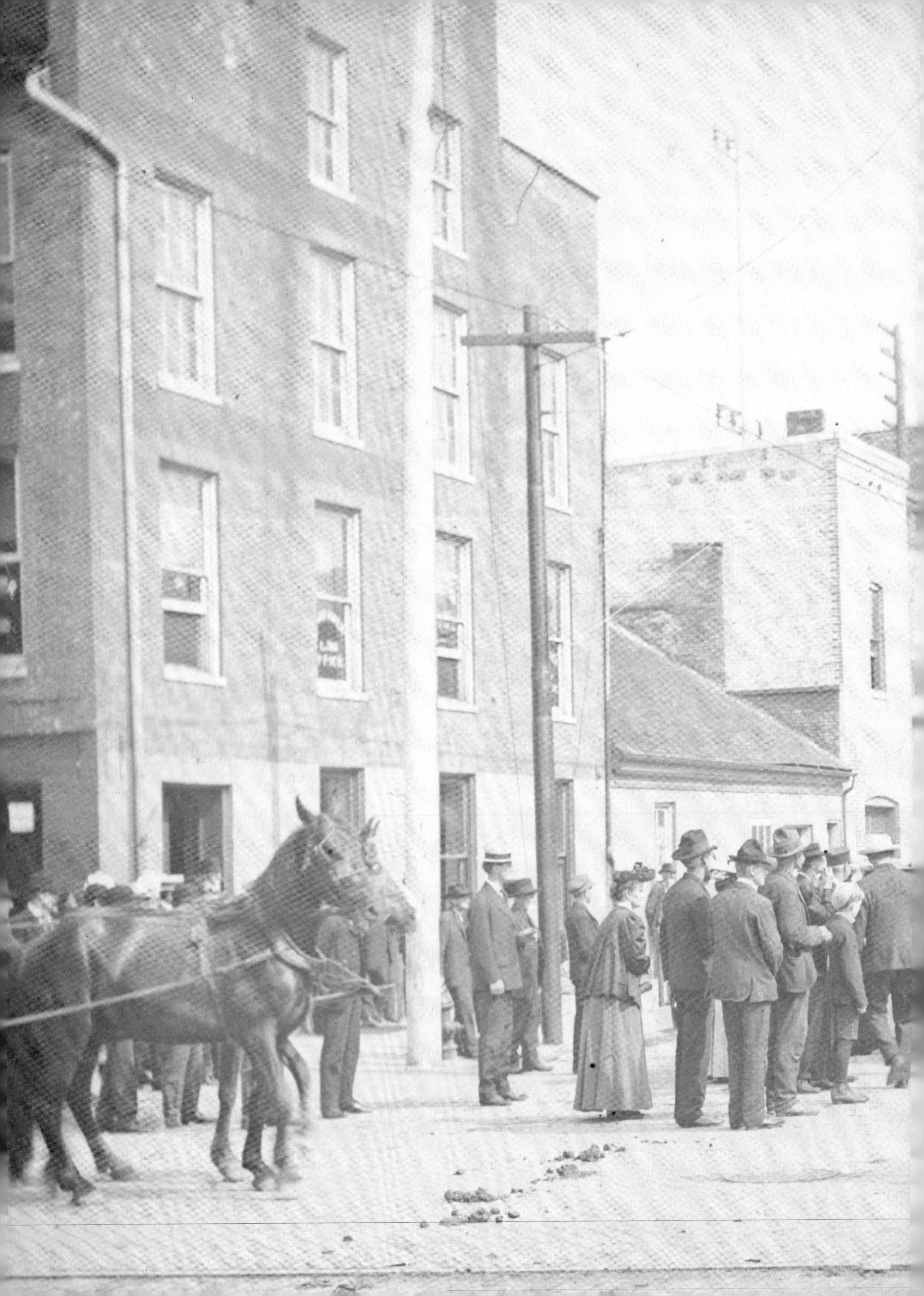

On July 4, 1906, Walter Smith (straw hat in center) and many others were waiting hopefully to board the crowded #304 Interurban to go somewhere to celebrate the holiday.

Ladies too made extensive use of the Interurban. Here the cars are stopped on Main in front of the Pike House at the southwest corner of Main and 4th.

Since the "cars", as they were called, provided frequent and relatively rapid service between two county seats, the Interurban replaced the old "Courthouse Flyer" of the Big Four line for commuting lawyers and businessmen. Newsboys also found the stations to be profitable places to "hawk" their papers.

This later postcard gives a view of the Niles station on 2nd Street.

The Interurban ran on a year 'round basis; or at least it tried to. Snowstorms which left snowdrifts like this could cause problems though.

This postcard shows a car streaking through the 2nd Street viaduct under the MCRR tracks.

The multi-pyloned bridge which allowed the Interurban to cross the Lake Chapin portion of the St. Joseph River south of Berrien Springs was touted as the longest interurban bridge in the world. Postcard views of it were a popular item.

139

Fire Department

The city's fire protection started as a bucket brigade. Individual property owners kept fire buckets at hand for emergency use. However, the inefficiency of the system, the combination of wooden buildings and the use of wood or coal for heat resulted in frequent and sometimes disastrous fires. As a result, in 1838 the citizens petitioned the Village Council for the organization of a fire company. Consequently, a volunteer company, "Niles Engine Company # 1," was organized. An "engine," as the hand operated pumps were called, was purchased, along with buckets, hoses, ladders, etc. However, the only source of water was private wells or the river. Cisterns were later constructed at several locations in the city, to collect rain water from the streets. This street run-off water while hardly clean was usable for firefighting.

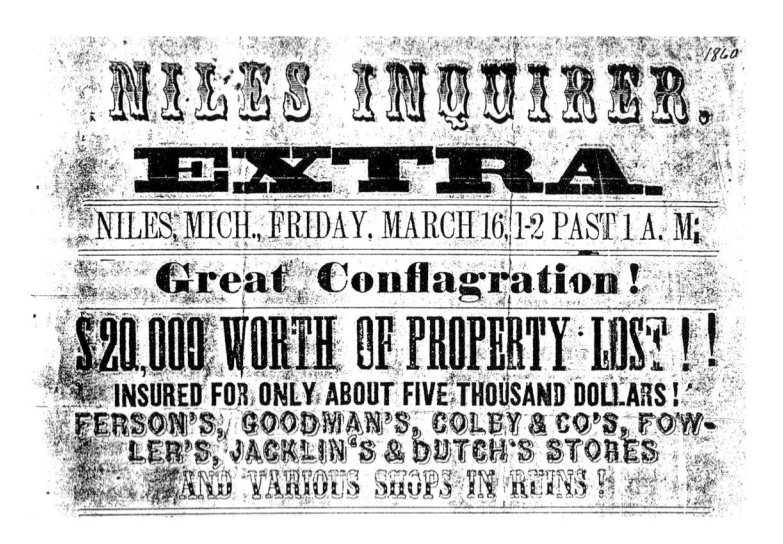

There was a reorganization in 1858 as a result of a large fire that nearly burned out a whole block of downtown.

Over the years as the city grew, other volunteer hose companies were added. They were made up of young athletic men, a necessity in the days of hand operated pumps and hand drawn carts. Eventually, Niles had four such companies who competed with each other in firefighting skills as well as in regular sports (their uniforms were the direct ancestors of baseball uniforms). By 1875, 15 officers and 175 men were serving as volunteers in the city's fire service.

In the 1890's a new central station was built in the 100 block on Sycamore Street. By 1903 the separate hose companies were terminated and the first paid fireman — a fire chief — was hired in 1908. With the purchase of the first truck and a hose carrier, in 1912 the department entered the modern era of firefighting.

Horse drawn rigs and the Central Station replaced the ward hose companies in the 1890's.

This handsome young man with a typical Victorian haircut was recruited not only for his firefighting skills, but also his athletic ability.

Officers of Lardner #2 with speaking trumpets and hose wrench.

Their chief, Art Coffinger, went on to become chief of all the Niles firemen in the early 1900's.

Men with one of the Niles volunteer hose companies all harnessed up for a practice run. Practice runs became a competitive sport. One area "all star" team sponsored by the Studebaker Company of South Bend which included several of Niles' best volunteers set the world's record — pulling their cart 200 yards, laying out 100 feet of hose, hooking it to the hydrant and spraying water — all in 34 seconds. Hose companies played a prominent part in parades with their carts decorated with flags and bunting.

The fire department obtained their first pumper truck, this 750 gallon American LaFrance, in 1923.

Fires like the complete destruction of the Galt House Hotel, in 1899, spurred the establishment of an up-to-date fire department with modern equipment. The Galt House Hotel, built in 1881 as the Bond House, stood on the northeast corner of Sycamore and 2nd streets.

As the fire department became more mechanized and as technology made their efforts more effective, the size of the department gradually grew smaller. By the 1980's, it had become a core of highly-trained professional firefighters, once again assisted by a group of dedicated volunteers. Another major change over the years was the addition of fire prevention activity to the responsibility for extinguishing fires. Inspecting for possible fire hazards, seeing that they are prevented, and educating the public about fire safety have become important tasks for the department as can be seen in this photo of a young Niles citizen during Fire Prevention Week in 1980.

BEAUTIFUL NILES

Niles has always been considered a scenic city and postcards of its tree-shaded streets, graceful bridges, and picturesque river banks have been popular for generations. This selection is from a glass plate negative archive from one of the local postcard makers.

POST OFFICE

When the village of Niles was first established, communications with the rest of the country were of primary importance. In 1829, Obed Lacey assumed the position of acting postmaster. In 1830, Isaac Grey was commissioned as the first official postmaster. In those days mail was carried on horseback or stagecoach (via the Detroit to Chicago Road) by private contractors, including several men from Niles. The first post office was undoubtedly in the Lacey General Store where residents called for their mail. After several moves, the post office in 1842 was located in a drugstore/newsstand/candystore on the corner of 2nd and Main. The post office patrons complained about

Picking up the morning mail at the post office at the corner of 3rd and Main was a welcomed part of the morning routine for the downtown businessmen, c. 1899.

In 1909, a new post office building was built on the southwest corner of 4th and Main. This new ultra modern building was the result of extensive lobbying by the Congressman E. L. Hamilton, who subsequently used his success at getting a new post office for Niles as a major campaign issue.

the number and "quality" of the people loitering on the premises and interfering with the post office business. This was resolved in 1889 with a new office being opened in the Gitchell building (corner 3rd and Main where Signal Travel is now located), which was strictly for postal use.

The 1909 post office served, with additions, for approximately 80 years. It was replaced in the early 1980's with a new building located on the old Central schoolgrounds. After standing vacant for a number of years, the 1909 post office building, now listed as a national historic site, is being restored and converted into offices.

Henry Lardner (Ring's older brother) was one of the city letter carriers in the early years of this century.

In the 1840s Rufus Landon was postmaster and the office was below Peak Hall on Main Sreet. He posted the following notice in the *Niles Intelligencer* in January of 1840:

POST OFFICE ARRANGEMENTS

Eastern mail closes daily at 1pm

Western mail closes daily at 7pm

Southern, every Sunday, Tuesday, and Friday at 7pm

Northern, every Wednesday at 7pm

St. Joseph every Monday and Thursday at 7pm

No credit will be given in any case whatever for postage

Letters claiming to be overcharged or having a less number of pieces must be opened in view of the postmaster or no abatement of postage can be allowed.

The inland postage on all letters sent to a foreign country must be paid in advance.

Newspapers, pamphlets and magazines, having any note or memorandum written on them will be charged with the letter postage. And all circulars, hand bills, lottery schemes, and prices current, with similar postage. Names on letters remaining to be picked up in the Post Office are published. Office hours; 7am to 8pm except Saturdays, when the office will be open from 9 to 10 am and from 1 to 2 pm and from 4 to 5 pm.

R. W. Landon, Postmaster

Postal work had always been considered "man's work," but in the the early 1920's Rose Gitchell Shockley (wife of rural letter carrier, Charles Shockley), became Niles' first female mail carrier.

Rural or outlying mail was delivered in horse-drawn vehicles screened with metal mesh for security in the warmer months. In the winter, sleighs and cutters were used until the 1920's & '30's.

☆ ☆ ☆ ☆ ☆ WORLD WAR I ☆ ☆ ☆ ☆

While World War I was short lived, the people from Niles were involved in various ways, at least in terms of the actual U.S. military participation.

While large numbers of men enlisted, relatively few saw actual combat in Europe. Most did their duty in this country. Some were still in training camps when the war ended. All of them shared the common experiences of basic training, sleeping "rough" or in pup tents, and the old "hurry up—and wait" in this case for dinner—or whatever passed for it.

As in all wars, the women had roles to play as well as the men. Niles area women registered to fill many civilian needs as well as serving overseas as nurses, ambulance drivers, and other non-combatant capacities.

The Memorial Day parade of 1919 was also a "homecoming" for the soldiers and sailors of Niles who had been serving their country.

NILES PUBLIC LIBRARY

The earliest libraries in Niles were privately owned. In 1881 the Ladies Library Association started a subscription library. People paid to join it and use the books. It had about 2,000 books and was located above a shoe store on the south side of Main Street between 2nd and 3rd streets. In 1883 the public schools also had a library available which was free to all residents of the City or of School District # 1 and to the pupils of the school.

The first public library was a Carnegie Library, one of many built in the country with funds provided by the industrialist, Andrew Carnegie. He provided $15,000 for the construction. Funds for furnishing and staffing were provided by the Federation of Club Women, various private donors and some support from the city. It opened to the public in 1904 with 5,000 books. It was replaced in 1963 when the library was moved to a new, larger modern structure at the corner of 7th and Main. By that time the collection of books had grown to over 33,000 and the old building could not hold it any more. Mrs. F. J. Plym donated nearly two million dollars to construct and furnish the new building.

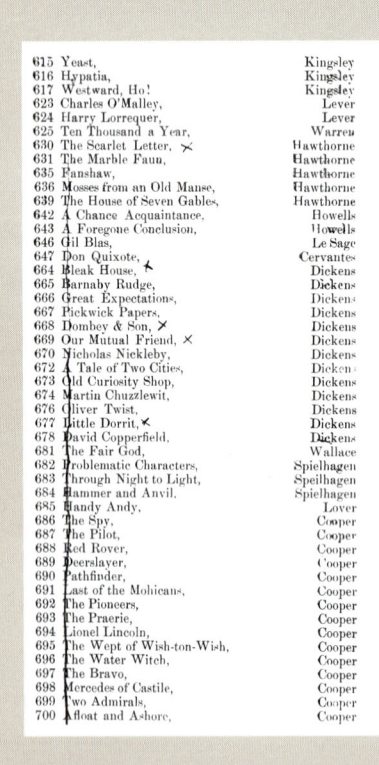

The 1883 school library catalogue listed all of the books available to be checked out.

The new Carnegie Library was designed by the Chicago architectural firm of Perkins and Robertson. One of a dwindling number of such buildings, it is a probable candidate for nomination to the Historical Register. This photo is of a postcard version of the architect's rendering.

The library was a significant symbol of community achievment as this popular Niles postcard depicting the "new" Carnegie Library shows.

Ring Lardner Jr. and other family members visited the Library to view an exhibit of their father and grandfather's publications during the Ring Lardner Centennial.

Photo of 1963 library.

SHOWTIME

In 1867 the Niles Opera House opened its doors ushering in three quarters of a century of live theatrical entertainment to the community. Niles also was the home base for several traveling troupes of showmen. One of the first was the group known as "The Peak Family Bell Ringers," the multi-talented family and friends of William Peak (who later operated the Opera House). They performed music, drama, comedy and acrobatic acts all over the country. Two of their "stars" who went on to fame on their own as adults, were Fannie Sutter Delano and Jeppe Delano.

John Stowe was well-known on the traveling show circuit. Pictured is his personal life-time free pass issued by "Buffalo Bill" Cody and Major G. W. "Pawnee Bill" Lillian to their shows. In addition to Stowe's road show there were several others who used Niles as their off season home.

In 1916 John Stowe directed and produced a version of *Uncle Tom's Cabin* using local talent. In the cast photo are many local notables who participated in order to raise funds for the new B.P.O.E Lodge (the Elks) which had just started in

PROGRAMME
FRIDAY AND SATURDAY EVENINGS
SPECIAL SATURDAY MATINEE FOR THE LITTLE FOLKS

UNCLE TOM'S CABIN
Produced Under the Direction of
JNO. F. STOWE
AUSPICES NILES LODGE NO. 1322
B. P. O. E.
BENEFIT HOME BUILDING FUND
BY HOME TALENT

Prologue written by Mrs. Eva Dinan Rosewarne.
Delived by Miss Mayme Baker

150

The Peak Family traveled under several different names, including the Peak Family Coronet Band. They had this elegant bandwagon built by the Elijah Murray Wagon Works of Niles for $600 to use in circus parades.

In 1903 two of Niles recent high school graduates collaborated in writing, scoring, and producing a minstrel show musical entitled *Zanzibar* for the town's amusement and edification. The writer, who in his script showed early signs of his comedic genius, was young Ring Lardner. According to the local papers the results of his efforts, and those of his partner, Harry Schmidt, were very well received by the community. In this cast photo young Ring, in black face make-up, is on the extreme left.

The Berrien Center Brass Band came by wagon to Niles to march in the grand 4th of July parade at the dedication of the Fort Saint Joseph Boulder in 1913.

Small orchestras like this provided the music in the local theaters and opera houses.

Brass bands such as the Mechanic's Band and the Niles Military Band enjoyed a tremendous increase in popularity in the post-Civil War period. Bands like these marched in the local parades and entertained on summer evenings at community bandstands built specifically for such purposes. The availability of such public entertainment was a desirable commodity when one was choosing the community in which one would raise a family in the years before the advent of radio.

THEATER

The "moving pictures" came to Niles in the very early years of the 20th century. The first movie theatres were small store front operations which showed the primitive, jerky films as a novelty. Because of their small size and ephemeral nature, they were called "match-box" theatres. While the names Mission, Isis, Royal, Star, Colonial, and People's are listed in early accounts of the town's theatres, few, if any, details are documented about their locations, years of existence, or operations. With the construction of the Riviera on 2nd Street by John Bauman in 1920, and the Ready on Main by T. W. Ready in 1927, the movies came of age in Niles. These two movie houses (which jointly cost $350,000 to build) represented a substantial investment in the entertainment of the town. They, along with the Strand Theatre, provided multi-faceted programs which combined traditional vaudeville with the new moving pictures ("talkies" after 1928) in a six or seven unit evening of entertainment for a 15 cent admission. The Strand, (located on Main next to the post office), failed to weather the Depression, and the Riviera closed in 1957, but the Ready in its remodeled and modernized form is still entertaining people with the silver screen.

In 1952 the Ready (part of the Butterfield group) was promoting its first-run movies and its air conditioning as well; while the independent Riviera, only five years away from closing, was featuring Gene Autry and lesser regarded stars.

Above: Located at the top of the Main Street hill across from the City Hall, at a major intersection, the Ready soon became a local landmark. The removal of the marquee in the early 1980's was a real loss to many who grew up in the town.

Right: Located on the west side of Second Street, around the corner from Main Street, the Riviera was convenient and popular, especially with the children of the town. The Ready may have attracted a more adult audience, but popcorn, serials, and cowboy movies at the Riveria are firmly fixed in the minds of several generations of Niles townsfolk. It is shown here in 1962 just before it and all of the adjacent structures were demolished in the name of "Urban Renewal."

Niles Police Department

Law enforcement in Niles was not considered to be a major municipal problem in the early years. It appears that most problems were handled locally and pretty much informally. The state legislation set up a justice of the peace and local constables. Major problems were handled by the county sheriff and his deputies. The 1851 Charter of the Village of Niles established the office of town marshall with the same powers as the state allowed to constables. The 1859 Charter of the City of Niles makes it clear that the marshal was to be the chief of the police, but it is not clear who the police were that he was the chief of. The constables were elected from each ward

Niles policeman Phillip Zwergal, c. 1890.

Niles' first police station was located at the corner of 2nd and Main streets. It was one of the first police departments in the area to have telephones installed in 1896. This little wood police station was moved in 1926 to 5th and Wayne where it was used by patrolmen working the north side of town. In 1955 it was retired to the F.O.P. Park where it is still in use.

Prohibition era police after breaking up a moonshine still in the Niles area.

156

and they were to work with the marshal. The marshal and constables were charged with enforcing the laws. This included collecting fines, executing various writs, and arresting violators.

A regular city police force was established in 1891 when former fireman George "Dude" Francis was appointed by the mayor as "night-watchman." In 1895 a small wooden building was erected at 2nd and Main and used as the police station. As other men were hired, "Dude" was promoted to town marshal and police chief, an office he held almost continually until his retirement in 1935.

The police station was moved to the south side of the intersection of 2nd, Front, and Broadway in 1926. The city bought the house that had been Dr. Smith's, then Dr. Carr's private hospital, and used it for the police. It was torn down for the police parking lot when the present day Public Safety Building was built in 1937-39.

Aftermath of police shootout in 1925.

Capt. Solloway with school kids, c.1955.

Local police at a crime scene.

157

THE CHAPINS

Henry Austin Chapin was a local merchant who came to Niles in 1846. He was involved in several businesses, first dry goods and then insurance, with moderate success. In his later years he acquired title to a piece of property in the Upper Peninsula of Michigan from his son-in-law. (Numerous legends have been coined to explain his ownership of the land). The land was examined by a team of mining engineers from Chicago who found that it was rich in iron ore. A company was then formed to mine the ore. The iron mine proved to be one of the richest in the nation's history, and Mr. Chapin became one of the wealthiest men in the state from his royalties. Millions of tons of ore were brought up over the years, and Mr. Chapin received a royalty fee of $.25 (later $.50) for each ton. Mr. Chapin and his son, Charles, used his money to become capitalists, investing it in new businesses and industries. They were among the founders of the Indiana and Michigan Electric Company.

In 1882 Mr. Chapin commenced building an elegant new home in Niles at the corner of 5th Street and Main Street. This new showplace was built in the finest style with the highest quality materials available. However the Chapins only lived in it for a few years. They soon relocated to Chicago where they lived on the "gold coast" along with others in their income range. They hired a local housekeeper for the Niles mansion and used it as a summer home. Mr.

Henry Austin Chapin, businessman, capitalist, millionaire.

The Chapin Mines (there were three actual mine shafts) were located in Iron Mountain in Michigan's Upper Peninsula. By the time it closed in 1932 the mine had produced over 27 million tons of ore. It was one of the largest and deepest iron mines in the world reaching down over 1500 feet. The mine was very wet and had to be constantly pumped to keep it from flooding. The pump used was the largest of its kind in the world and is still standing as a historical monument. The mines themselves collapsed a few years after they were shut down and the resulting crater flooded to form a lake.

Chapin died in 1898. The mansion was used less and less by the family, though they still had relatives and business interests in the area. It was used on occasion for community services, and at least once the third floor ballroom was used for a high school dance.

In the 1930's the vacant home was sold to the city for the token fee of $300 (probably about enough to cover the legal costs of the transaction) by the surviving Chapin grandchildren. The sale stipulated that the mansion and its carriage house and boiler house had to always be used for city purposes. It is this condition which has probably been the only thing that has preserved the buildings.

The city, using WPA labor, converted the mansion into a city hall. This was done with minimal alterations. A few years later the former carriage house and boiler house were remodeled to provide a building for the city's museum, the Fort Saint Joseph Museum, which opened in 1939. Though some structural changes were required, the house is still mostly original and is about 95% restorable. At least one of the offices, the former library, has been partially restored for the office of the city administrator.

The Chapin Mansion is typical of the wealthy builders of the late Victorian period. It combines elements of many architectural styles grafted in an eclectic manner onto a house of basic Queen Anne proportion. Though designed by the noted society architects Wheelock & Clay, it is probably more a reflection of the Chapins newly acquired wealth than the architect's taste. It has a basement and three floors, the uppermost being a ballroom with high vaulted ceilings. It is lavishly finished with ornately carved woodwork, copious amounts of stained glass, and each of the major rooms has an elegant fireplace mantle of fine wood and marble. Even fifty years of use as city offices with office furniture, carpet, lighting and institutional paint have failed to extinguish its former ostentatious splendor, dimmed it perhaps, but not extinguished it.

Automobiles

As elsewhere, the invention and popular application of the internal combustion engine made radical changes in the community. The automobile changed the pace of life. Until it came along, life was geared to the speed of a horse. Railroads and steamboats existed and were used extensively, but only along fixed routes. Bicycles, though very popular, while allowing great individual freedom of movement were severely restricted by weather (and their owners' physical limits).

Automobiles, and other such vehicles, (once they were past the first experimental years), provided rapidity of travel previously unimaginable, in almost all types of weather; and personal freedom in that they were not restricted to rails or rivers. When mass production methods made the cost of automobiles accessible to the average family, a transformation of American society began to take place.

Though horses and autos would co-exist on Niles streets for many years to come, things began to change when Dr. C. P. Hanson purchased the first documented automobile in Niles in 1901. It was this Oldsmobile runabout in which the proud owner, his wife, and daughter are posing. It cost about $750, more than a year's wages for the average worker and was literally little more than a horseless carriage.

In just a few short years automobile made drastic improvements. In 1907 Bascom Parker (a local businessman and Ring Lardner's first boss) and a group of his cronies were using this much improved automobile to make pleasure jaunts. In this photo dated September 15, 1907, they were setting out from Niles to go to Buffalo, New York.

With the rapid acceptance of the auto came the necessary services to maintain them. Here is "gasoline alley" Niles-style. This is the interior of Fred Babcock's Auto Repair Service at 13th and Main streets in the early years. It appears that "borrowed" tools were as big a problem for mechanics then as now.

Mr. M. Z. Mell obtained the city's first taxi license and by 1917, the date of this photo, operated an automobile livery service. Here are some of his vehicles parked at the MCRR depot awaiting passengers.

161

Trucks soon replaced horse-drawn wagons for deliveries as well. This World War I era delivery truck belonging to the one of National Printing and Engraving Company is believed to be one of the first trucks in the city.

As the years progressed and the auto became more and more popular, a number of auto dealerships were established in Niles that sold both new and used cars. Noble Pontiac had a range of cars from 1924 to 1938 models available at their dealership on Sycamore between 4th and 5th streets according to this 1938 photo.

Motorized bicycles were also popular with the more adventurous. This pre-World War I motorcycle is typical of the earliest versions.

During World War II auto production ceased in order to produce material needed for the war effort. Consequently, after the war, automobiles were in short supply. Many returning servicemen like Ira Clark, purchased motorcycles like his 1945 Harley-Davidson for inexpensive, but available transportation in the immediate post-war years.

As the car took over the major transportation role, the community physically changed to adapt to it. Streets were widened and paved, making the removal of many trees necessary. Old bridges were replaced with wider stronger structures. Parking became a problem in the downtown shopping area — more space was required since nearly everyone had a car to park. Consequently, many of the older buildings were demolished to provide parking lots. Brick streets, which became dangerously slippery when wet or frosty and were too uneven and rough for the higher speeds of the autos, were replaced with concrete or covered over with asphalt. Gas stations began replacing the neighborhood corner stores, though in later years they too started selling food and grocery items as convenience stores.

NILES AIRPORT

The earliest days of aviation in Niles are difficult to track. Itinerant "barn-stormer" pilots visited Niles off and on over the early years, attracting large crowds to see their exploits. In 1925, the first regular landing field was opened by several local businessmen. The open area on the southeast corner of Lake and 17th streets, now used by the Apple Festival and the school bus facility, was set aside for that purpose. Early airports were simply flat, grassy fields, with room enough to take off and land the airplanes of that era. Several World War I veteran pilots and their "jenny" planes operated from the airport. In 1930, the Heath Aircraft Company moved to Niles from Chicago. Heath built airplanes in buildings where Simplicity Pattern is now located. Between 1930 and 1934, when Mr. Heath was killed in a crash, more than 100 planes were built in Niles. During that period the frame buildings Heath used were moved to Lake Street and additional land acquired by the city to form the present day airport.

The airport was named in memory of Jerry Tyler, the founder of Tyler Refrigeration Company of Niles, who was killed along with his family in a Chicago hotel fire. Many of Niles' industries have owned or based company planes at the airport over the years. It is now city owned and facilities are rented to both corporate and private pilots.

Over the years the interest in flying in the Niles area has led to the establishment of several flying schools to train private pilots. This 1930's postcard shows several of the bi-planes then available for lessons.

This photo is considered to be a picture of the first airplane, a very early Wright-type plane, to visit Niles.

In this aerial picture of the early airport, c. 1930, the bi-planes are old "jennys". The single wing craft are locally made Heath Parasols. The Parasol was one of the first commercially made monoplanes. The crowd is gathered for an airshow along 17th Street where the present Apple Festival grounds are located.

164

The Niles Aviation School had several of these World War I veteran "jennys" to train in.

This has been identified as one of the Heath Parasols made here in Niles.

This low-wing monoplane is fairly typical of the private planes to be found at the Niles airport around the middle of the century.

Zepplins were another type of aircraft to shadow the skies over the area. This photo, and many postcards, show the *Graf Zepplin* as it flew over the Interurban bridge at Berrien Springs.

165

Donavon Smith

Niles boys were fascinated with early aviation. Actually having planes built in Niles, seeing them take off and land right at the edge of town, and having the "the fearless men" visible on the streets of town, stimulated the imagination of many. One man who put his dreams to work was Donavon Smith. In the late '30's and early '40's, he, along with other airplane crazy boys, built models and flew them along the edges of the airport. He graduated from Niles High School in 1940 and enlisted in the air corps in early '42. A year later, he was flying combat missions over Europe. Flying B-47's, he became one of the youngest "aces" in the theatre. He was credited with shooting down six Nazi fighters, including three in one day. For this feat he was awarded the Distinguished Service Cross; just one of the many decorations he received. He stayed in the Air Force after the war. He became one of the early jet pilots. He retired from the Air Force in 1973 as a Lt. general. A park in Niles which is known as veterans park is actually the Lt. Gen. Donavon F. Smith Veterans Memorial Park.

Photo taken from dedication of General Smith's park brochure.

Picture of painting of Smith's B-47.

Don Smith as a youngster with his gasoline engine model airplane

Ostrander's Store

Lloyd W. Ostrander opened the Ostrander Grocery Store in 1919 on what was then a country lot in Niles. His store was fairly typical of the many neighborhood grocery stores which served the city in the pre-supermarket era, with one exception. Since he was an avid fisherman, he also kept a stock of fishing supplies in addition to his regular inventory of grocery items. After many years, he retired and turned the business over to his son, Lloyd M. Ostrander who operated it for many more years. Though the grocery store is now gone, the building is still standing today.

1931

OSTRANDER'S
1438 Oak Street   We Deliver   Phone 699
SATURDAY, JUNE 4
Niles Golden Bonus Jubilee Tickets Here
YOU MAY WIN A PLYMOUTH, CHEVROLET OR ROCKNE

Prime Baby Beef Roast, lb.	13c	Butter, Good Creamery, lb.	19c
Veal Sirloin or Round, lb.	18c	Native Veal Shoulder, lb.	15c
Pork Loin Roast, Lean	11c	Good Sliced Bacon, 2 lbs.	19c

GOLDEN BONUS JUBILEE GROCERIES

Fresh String Beans, 2 lbs.	15c	Head Lettuce Medium, 2 for	15c
Borden's Chateau Sandwich Cheese	14c	Sweet Potatoes 5 lbs. for	17c
Little Elf Salmon, 2 cans	23c	Big Calument pkg. Cocoanut	29c
Large Package Oats Contains Glassware 1 Package	19c	FREE handy measuring scoop with each regular 25c package of AIRY FAIRY KWIK-BIS-KIT	25c. pkg
Tall Can Jerzee Milk, Sat, 4 cans	25c		
Olivilo Soap Regular at 9c, Saturday, Four Bars	25c		

This 1931 flyer advertises the sale items. It also notes the Jubilee tickets which offered a chance to win a Plymouth, Chevrolet, or Rockne automobile.

Many of the neighborhood stores delivered groceries to the customer's homes. Local boys found their first employment delivering groceries for the corner store. Very early though, the Ostranders acquired a truck for the business. Here it is shown on its way to a customer who is content to wait for his or her groceries to arrive at the door.

The Ostrander store was located on the southeast corner of 15th and Oak streets. This photo shows the store as it looked just after a 1935 remodeling. Stores such as this one, where the owner and his family lived upstairs over the shop, were small, intimate, comfortable places where the customer was probably known by his or her first name; and the friendliness and congenial honesty of the storekeeper and his family were a pleasant break from the household and workplace chores and duties.

NILES HIGH SCHOOL

In the earlier days of the Niles educational system "schooling" meant not only the 3-R's but also good posture, good manners, elocution and oratory skills, and of course good penmanship. In fact, while one was rewarded by grades in school for one's handwriting skills, in later life elegant penmanship was an important job skill as well as one of the attributes whereby one's upbringing, education, and general finesse in life would be judged.

The male students competed in sports and academic achievment; preparing themselves for graduation and subsequent life as a bread-winner for their family. Few found it necessary to entertain thoughts of higher education or advanced training.

The women were trained through our school system primarily to be homemakers, housewives, and mothers. Occasionaly they might work outside the home but usually that was only until they married.

Niles Educatio

The few socially accepted exceptions were the girls who ventured off to "Normal" school to become teachers or nurses. Even more exceptional (if not rare) was the girl who went to college for training to become a physician.

As society in America has evolved, so has the educational system in Niles. Gone are the old homemaker-oriented home economics classes which provided instruction in cooking, sewing, and child care. Today they have been replaced with career and job-oriented classes.

Dance-cards are long gone, totally unknown to generations who relate better to compact discs and electronic keyboards. For today's student, educational plans which include college or other advanced training are the norm rather than the exception. Sports, music, drama, and dance, are still important and popular components of the educational experience though they all bear the noticeable and far-reaching evidence of the changes in cultural and social values in the community over the years.

In 1941 the Niles Educational Tour, made up of students, teachers and friends had their photo taken posed in front of the nation's Capitol.

Niles High School

Above left: Early view of the school grounds leading up to Union School. The grounds were not only used for school activities, but public and civic as well.

Above Right: Niles High School as seen from Main Street.

Left: View of the facade of Central School located on Boradway.

In May of 1956 a whole new Niles High School was completed. Construction cost more than $2 million but it gave the city a state-of-the-art school complete with athletic fields.

170

In the years before World War I, baseball was the American pastime. The Niles High School team posed for this formal team portrait. The community also supported the Niles "Blues," the popular semi-professional local practitioners of the sport.

The 1906 N.H.S. football team posed in front of the Civil War cannon which stood on the Main Street side of the school.

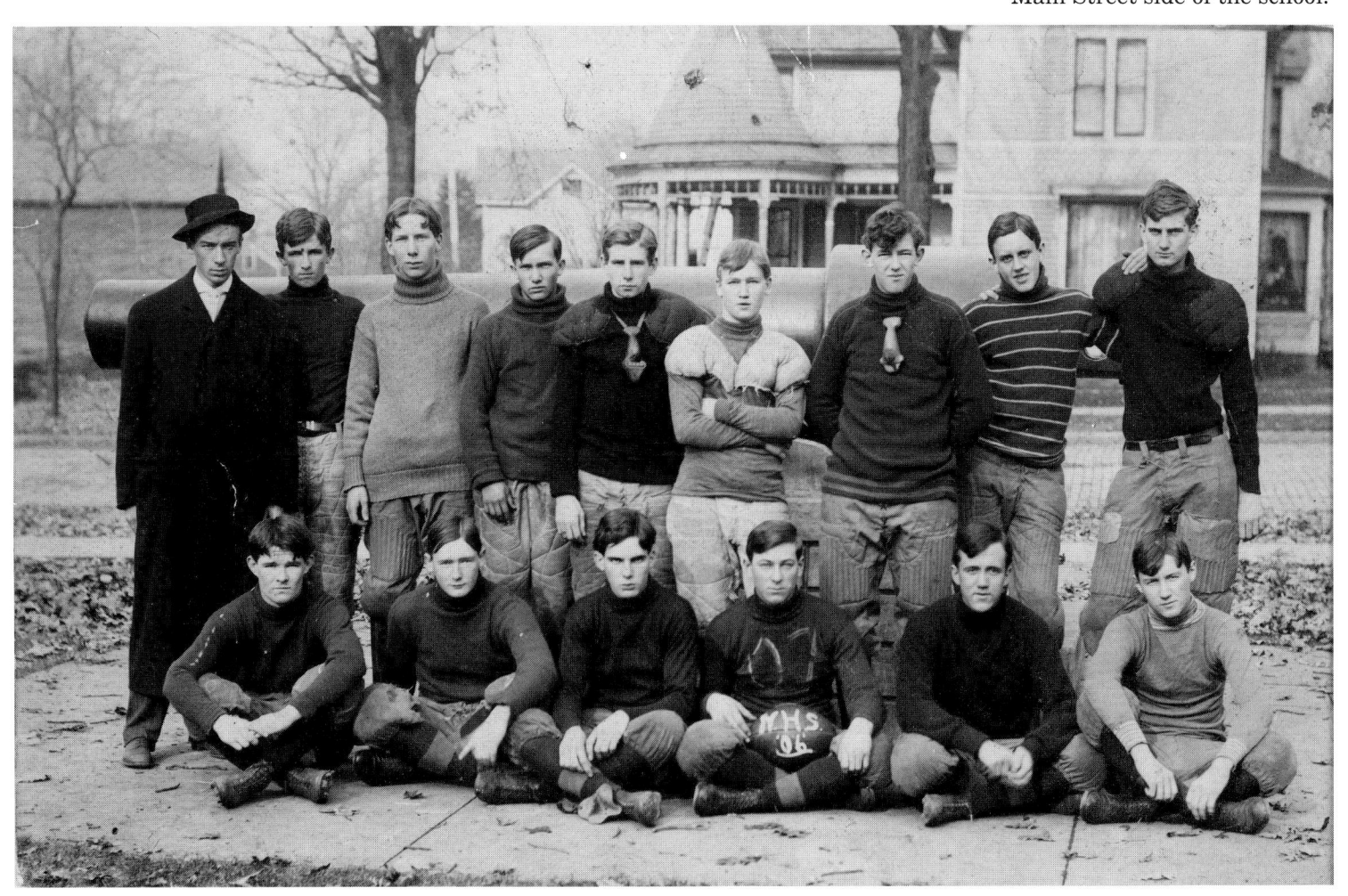

171

Niles High School

In 1917 the high school formed its own reserve Army Corps for military training. This is a photo of the 1919 group.

In 1922 an Armistice Ball was held to celebrate the 10th anniversary of the end of World War I.

In 1922 and again in 1942 the N.H.S. basketball team won the state wide championship for Class-B size schools. The '22 team had a record of 25 victories without a defeat.

In 1951, upon completion of their first unbeaten—untied season, the Niles Vikings football team were the "unofficial" Class "B" State Champions.

Basketball games have always been a big crowd pleaser. This photo shows the very first "jump ball" in the new high school gymnasium.

The Niles High School Band has long been known for being both big and good. It has often received a number one rating in band competitions. Half-time at the football games gave the N.H.S. Band a chance to play and to form their popular "N-for-Niles" formation.

NILES HIGH SCHOOL

The 1956 "Snow Ball" was the first to be held in the new cafeteria. It was presided over by King Jim Cousins and Queen Patty Cottrel.

King Jim Cousins and Queen Patty Cottrel.

The traditional Grand March Finale drew many couples out onto the floor at the Prom in 1964.

Each year the prom took on a particular theme. In 1964 "Crystal Castle" was the chosen theme. The students and their dates danced to the music of "Dif and his Orchestra." Note both the short and long gowns, strapless dresses, and long gloves that were part of "proper attire."

Before the days of the health food craze, the candy store in the hall across from the auditorium was a great place to stock up on "smoothies" and "chico sticks."

Coach Ed Weede was, for many years, synonymous with sports at N.H.S.

Mr. George Flora was a N.H.S. music tradition.

Patty Robinson was a familiar sight and a spectacular baton twirler at all home and away games.

Tommy (James) Jackson as a N.H.S. student worked at the Spin-It Record Shop; which would someday be selling his national hit record "Hanky Panky."

175

Private Schools of Niles

Niles has always prided itself in the high quality of education available for its young people. In addition to the public school system, the community, over the years, has offered a selection of private schools. The Catholic elementary school dates back to the late 1800's. In the early 1960's the Seventh Day Adventist Church built a private elementary school. And in September of 1980 the First Assembly of God Church opened a new elementary and high school just outside the eastern city limits. It has educated students from as many as 70 different area churches. Over the past 150 years a number of other private schools have operated in the community.

First Assembly Christian School.

St. Mary's Catholic Elementary School

The Westside Seventh Day Adventist Elementary School.

Chapter V

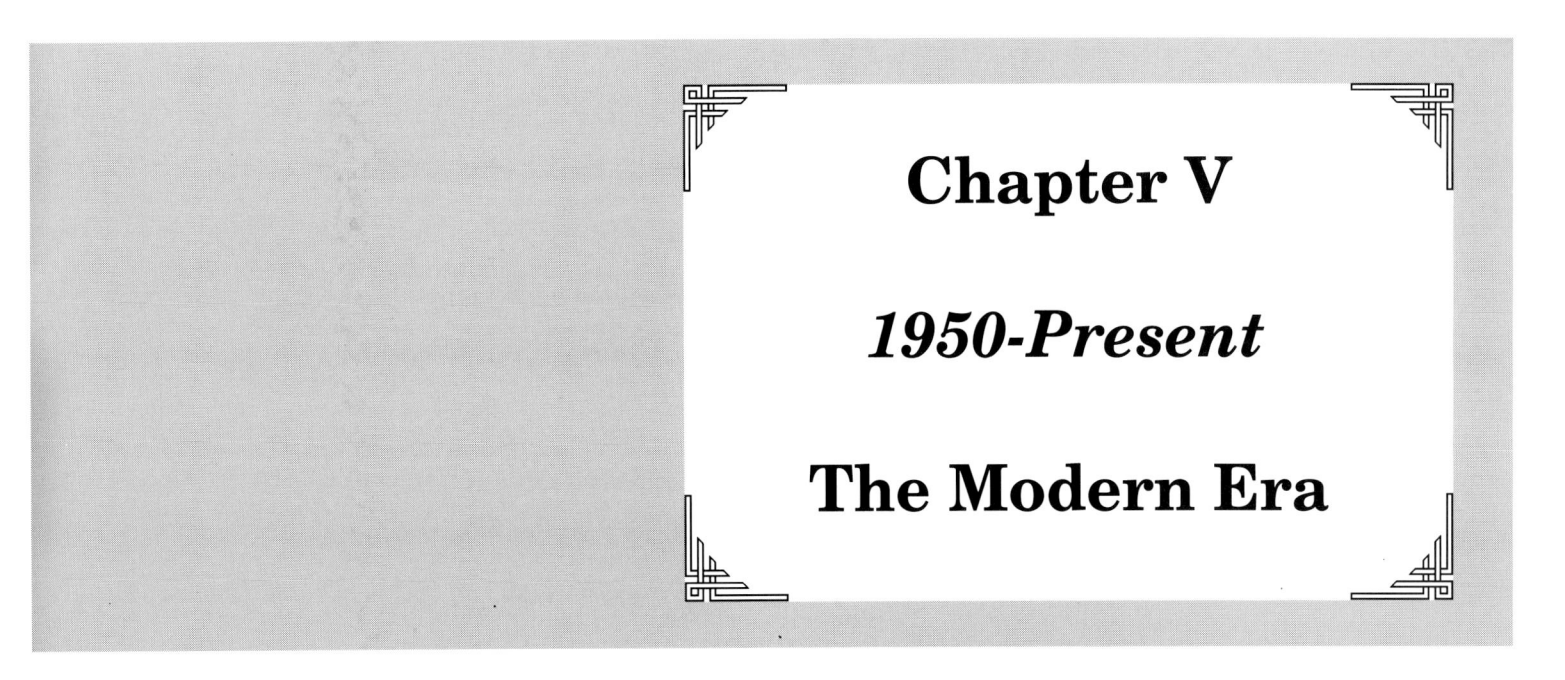

1950-Present

The Modern Era

The post-World War II period began with great hope. The men were back home and the industries of Niles were in good shape from the war effort. During the first part of this era, the community expanded its economic base. New schools were built to accommodate the post-war population boom as were, new homes and businesses. Niles was an industrial town and proud of it. In fact, one of the national news magazines is reputed to have labeled Niles as the "most industrialized city, on a per capita basis, in the nation." While this reference may be apocryphal it accurately reflects the towns self-perception. However circumstances were about to seriously alter the community. Most of the problems were the result of national economic changes, however some earlier decisions at the local level contributed to the problems which were about to overwhelm the town.

Factors which affected the whole nation and region had a tremendous impact on the local community. Things such as aging production facilities, increased labor costs, failure to anticipate market changes, and new taxes needed to finance aggressive social programs combined to turn the industrial north into the "rust belt." At the same time the southern states were offering incentive packages, tax abatements, and a large non-union labor pool to attract industries to the "sun belt." In the 1960s and 70s some local industries moved south, producing a devastating effect on the community. While almost all of the industrialized Northeast was effected by this to some degree, Niles was especially hard hit. Most of the industries were locally owned, but some of them had come under the control of public stockholders and professional managers with no loyalty to the local community. In other cases it was a matter of corporate survival. A major company, Kawneer, had fallen under control of outside corporate conglomerate ownership. They succumbed to the "sun belt" temptation. In the mid-1980s their now abandoned real estate and buildings were donated to the City as a property tax saving measure.

Niles was dealt another major shock in the mid-1950s. The railroad, one of the largest employers, shut down its facilities and moved them to Elkhart, Indiana. While many families recalls with anger the job losses that the relocation caused, in reality the railroad had been in a decline for years. The end of war-time transportation needs, the advent of the "super-highway" system and increasing truck usage cut heavily into rail traffic, as did the resumption of passenger car production.

The loss of Kawneer and the railroad yard and shops caused a reduction in tax revenue which financed local government at a time when increasing population, expanding social programs, and inflation were making greater demands on it. In turn, this forced a reduction in the level and quality of services available to the community.

While similar conditions could be found anywhere in the Northeast, another factor caused Niles further problems. The proximity of Niles to the Indiana-Michigan state line and the differential between the tax and business laws of the two states caused some service businesses and numerous property owners to move to Indiana while continuing to work in the Niles area, thus removing additional payroll from the local economy.

The downtown area rebounded well however. At its nadir in the mid-70s one would have seen a large number of vacant store fronts and a large open area which had been urban renewed. As of the writing (1990-91) that situation has changed. Now when stores become vacant they are reoccupied fairly quickly. New speciality shops have opened. Once again the town is beginning to capitalize on its location as a business asset. This time it is being marketed as a recreational and leisure activity area for the major metropolitan areas which surround it, particularly the Chicago market. Of special significance has been the development of the "antique mall" concept (a number of antique shops set up as a cooperative under one roof). These ventures have been very successful in Niles and have inspired a number of imitators in the area. The restaurants, fishing and boating, cultural and sports activities, as well as the beautiful environment are attracting a larger number of visitors each year. Once again the St. Joseph River is being recognized as one of the community's major economic assets, as it has been for the last three centuries.

While some remember with fondness the old days when industrial employment was Niles, there is a developing awareness that the community's future lies less in the area of industrial development and more in the improvement of the "quality of life."

HISTORY OF NILES BANKING

Banking in Niles prior to the 20th century ranged from the "wildcat banks" of the 1830's, to the three state and federal chartered banks of the 1860's and 1870's. All three types eventually failed causing great losses to depositors and rate holders.

The exception to these bank failures was a private bank established by Rodney C. Paine in 1852 that conducted a reliable business until his death in 1875 with no known losses to depositors.

The era of dependable and trustworthy banking in Niles began in 1901 when a private bank was formed by W.W. Newman and Richard Snell on March 23 and the Niles City Bank (a state chartered bank) that opened for business on July 3rd. These two banks continued in business through several name and charter changes until the state and national bank holidays of February and March 1933.

The Newman and Snell private bank was reorganized under a state charter in 1916, changed its name to State Bank of Niles in the 1920's, discontinued business in 1944 and sold its assets to the First National Bank in 1945.

The Niles City Bank located in a small building on the south side of Main Street in the same area now occupied by the Old Kent Bank-Southwest. On April 1, 1929, this bank was converted to a National Bank and was named the City National Bank and Trust Company. In 1932 it became a member of the Guardian Detroit Union group by an exchange of stock.

After the state and national bank holidays of

The former Paine Bank Building is considered by architectural historians to be one of the finest commercial Greek Revival style buildings in the country. It was built by R. C. Paine as the office for his bank in the mid 1840's. It was initially located on Main Street near the northwest corner of 3rd and Main. It was moved around the corner in the late 1800's to a new location on Third Street where it housed a number of different businesses until 1964. It is illustrated in this late 1940's photo in its second location being used as a gift and antique shop.

In 1964 it was threatened with demolition to make way for a new city parking lot. It was aquired and relocated by private owners in order to preserve it. It now stands at 1008 1/2 Oak Street. It is the only building in Niles listed in the prestigious survey of Historic American Buildings (HABS) and is most probably the oldest still existing bank building in Michigan.

This photo from the 1891 book of Niles photos is entitled *Picturesque Niles* by Frank H. Nix. It shows the interior of the Citizen's National Bank. The elegant but subdued mahogany and brass furnishings were designed to create an aura of substance and respectability.

178

February and March 1933, the City National Bank and Trust Company was declared insolvent and placed under a conservator. The officers and directors then formed a new bank that opened August 21, 1933, in the same location and named it First National Bank of Niles. On October 1, 1966, the name was changed to First National Bank of Southwestern Michigan.

The Western Michigan Corporation, a bank holding company, was formed in July 1975 and it then acquired the First National Bank of Southwestern Michigan by an exchange of stock. Western Michigan Corporation was merged into Pacesetter Financial Corporation on February 1, 1978.

Pacesetter Financial Corporation was acquired by Old Kent Financial Corporation in April, 1983, so the name of the Niles bank was then changed to Old Kent Bank-Southwest. It is the largest bank in southwestern Michigan with branches in Buchanan, Berrien Springs, St. Joseph, Benton Harbor area, Sodus, Dowagiac, Cassopolis and six Niles area locations.

Since 1971, branches have been opened in Niles by banks located in other parts of Michigan—American Bank of Kalamazoo, Michigan National Bank of Bloomfield Hills, First Commercial Savings of Cassopolis and the Community State Bank of Dowagiac. Of these, only the Community State Bank, now named FMB Community Bank, and the First Commercial Savings Bank, now named Michigan National Bank-Michiana still exist.

During this span of years, many state and national laws have been passed to better control banking for the protection of depositors. The next 154 years should show a much improved record over the past.

In this Civil War era picture of the northeast corner of second and Main, another of Niles early banks is visible in the corner building. Little is known about the Colby's Bank and it was probably very short lived since the Citizens National took over the building in the late 1860's. At the right hand margin of the photo one may see the side of the Paine Bank building. In the basement, below the bank, with an outside sidewalk stairway entrance is one of the town's oyster bars.

In this later, but still early, photo the Citizens National Bank has taken over and remodeled the Colby Bank quarters. The oyster bar is gone and a more businesslike front has been built. It was most likely at this time that the interior shown on the preceding page was constructed.

WORLD WAR II

Niles was intimately involved in World War II; not only did many of its young men join the military services, but the townsfolk also participated. They bought bonds to finance the war, sacrificed gas, candy, stockings and many other rationed items and gave up many metallic objects for the "scrap drives." The industries also lent their time, ability and skill to the war effort. While some local industries pre-war products were usable in the "Arming of Democracy," others adapted their machinery and production lines to new products of a military nature. For instance, Simplicity Pattern turned its printing facilities to the production of, among other things, targets used to teach soldiers to shoot. It is possible that many of the young men from Niles learned to shoot at targets printed in their own hometown. At least one former Simplicity employee is known to have found himself shooting at targets he himself had helped print a few weeks earlier.

Here are four randomly chosen snapshots representative of the men from Niles who served. Shown (top to bottom) are Edward Walker III, John F. Gipner, Robert A. Robbins, and Ted Millard.

While most of the men returned, some did not...

CITATIONS

will be presented by the Honorable William Morgridge, Mayor of the City of Niles, to mothers, wives and next of kin to the boys who have made the supreme sacrifice for our country:

FREDERICK P. AMON
PVT. HENRY HANCOCK
CORP. WILLIAM G. HALSTEAD
ENSIGN WILLIAM LEA OWEN
ROBERT CAIN
JOSEPH KOOLS
PVT. LEROY E. ANDE
MICHAEL ORIAS, JR.
CORP. JOSEPH L. KLIMEK
PVT. LAWRENCE W. LEHR
CAPT. HARRY L. WALTERS
PVT. CLARENCE STOOPS
SGT. DUANE COLE
ERNEST DOHM
CORP. DONALD C. DUNIFIN
PVT. CHARLES KIRK
STAFF SGT. JOHN KONKEY
GEORGE H. MILLER
JOHN A. SHOOK
STAFF SGT. WALTER HAYES
SGT. ROBERT REPINE
STAFF SGT. RICHARD W. SHIPPERLEY
GORDON FORD ROHLFS
ROBERT DUNN
PVT. ROBERT RILEY
RICHARD H. STRONG
TECH. SGT. JAMES L. CURTIS
TECH. SGT. CLAYTON KISTE
JOSEPH E. HAASE
PFC. RUSSELL B. JARRELL
PVT. LEO CURTIS
LIEUT. CLIFFORD I. JAYSON
STAFF SGT. CLELAND W. AMON
PFC. ROBERT OCHENRYDER
STAFF SGT. WILLIAM M. HAASE
STAFF SGT. RAY HENDERSON
PVT. GEORGE MARKS
PFC. GEORGE NICHOLSON
PFC. KEITH WORSTER
PVT. HENRY GINDER
PFC. JOSEPH H. DOUGLAS
PFC. CALVIN E. ALLEN
PFC. ROBERT TENNYSON
CPL. ROBERT S. MORRIS
LIEUT. KEITH BEALL
CPL. JAMES YARRICK
PVT. RAYMOND JOHNSON
PVT. WILLIAM B. CASPER
STAFF SGT. WILLIAM J. CALLAHAN
SGT. VICTOR HARTLINE
PFC. DONALD BLANK
STAFF SGT. FRANK ELO
PFC. E. L. ALBERT
PVT. AARON J. FRIZZELL
PFC. DONALD DAWSON
PVT. DUANE E. LARSON
SGT. HOWARD ARMSTRONG
CORP. HOWARD NELSON
CORP. JESSE SISK
PVT. KENNETH LINVILLE
S. SGT. GORDON KLINE
T. SGT. W. GHOLSON BOGGS

During the war many of the service organizations attempted to provide aid and assistance to the servicemen and their families.

The Niles Lions Club set up this servicemen's pickup shelter on the boulevard in front of city hall.

Left: "Rosie the Riveter" helped wartime Kawneer produce over 300 different aircraft sub-assemblies.

Right: Many women found work during the war in production lines that had been previously "men-only" employment. Here a woman is installing fluorescent lights in Tyler's food refrigeration cases.

Looking up Main Street from 2nd, five minutes after the end of the War with Japan was publicly announced—World War II was officially over. With the rationing of gas to be a thing of the past hundreds of cars, and Nilesites, paraded up and down the main thoroughfare until the wee hours of the morning. The fighting was over and most of the boys were coming home.

181

CITY DEPARTMENTS

The care and maintenance of the city's streets have always been a major concern of the citizens and a responsibility of the elected officials. One of the primary problems in the past was that the city's main street was on a hill. In the spring when the thaw came it became nearly unusable. When the street was covered with bricks in 1901 it was considered a highly significant sign of community improvement, as was the covering over of the old bumpy bricks by a later generation.

This April Fool's Day snow was not too much of a hazard to horses in 1899; but a few years later the streets would be treacherous for automobiles when snow and ice glazed the bricks. This danger led to the demand for the replacement of the brick surfaces with concrete or asphalt.

The bricking crew at work in early September 1902. Most of the street is done all the way to the top of the hill, except for the area around the streetcar tracks. Note the brick piles along the sidewalks. While the work was done by a contractor, many of the Niles high school boys worked as helpers, carrying bricks, grading the sand bed the bricks were laid on, and pouring on and sweeping in the sand which filled the gaps between the bricks.

This illustrates the last step in the process of the brick paving of Main Street. Fine sand was poured with the long handled funnels into the cracks. Then it was brushed in and soaked to lock the bricks into place.

For many years horses and automobiles co-existed on the streets of Niles. Behind the city's horse-drawn water wagon which is sprinkling down the dust of the street, one can see both a buggy and an early automobile. This glass plate negative photo probably dates from 1915.

During the Depression, the Works Progress Administration (WPA) and similar agencies provided the manpower needed to accomplish many local projects for the public benefit. The remodeling of the Chapin mansion into a city hall, conversion of the Chapin's carriage house into a museum and similar work was helpful; but digging ditches and installing new storm sewers, as in this photo, was more common work.

Prior to the bricking itself, a lot of preliminary work such as ditching to bury drainage lines had to be done. This photo shows one of the turn-of-the-century street improvement crews (contractors, not city employees) busy leaning on their shovels.

SMALL BUSINESSES

Right: Though it was to be dismantled and rebuilt on Bathhouse Row in Hot Springs National Park, Hot Springs, Arkansas in the late 1980's, the Paris Candy Shop was a "coming of age" place for many of the youngsters of Niles. Generations of people returned to attempt to locate their names, along with those of their sweethearts, carved (hopefully unnoticed) in one of the dark wooden booths. A family owned business for many years this candy store was also the local downtown gathering place for businessmen and women to take morning coffee and catch upon the latest news. In this photo, second generation owner and candy maker, Ted Patterson, is being photographed by a local newspaper photographer as he prepares to make the final batch of his justly famous hand made Christmas candy canes.

Roegers Candy Store on Main Street, c 1890.

In 1913-14 the Fisher Family had "just" pride in their new bakery located in the 200 block of Main Street.

In the 1890's the City Shoeing Shop (for shoeing horses) and Bolton & Wyant's wood and coal yard were to be found on the west side of Front Street just around the corner from Main.

Since 1839 Dean's Drug Store has located on Main Street.

The W. L. Babbitt Lumber Company was located on Front Street about where Area Lumber is now located; at least that is where it was until it was destroyed in a spectacular fire—one of the last major fires in the downtown area.

The J & E Woodruff store on the northwest corner of Front and Main where Beeson's had previously operated a store.

The Globe Dining Hall was obviously very proud of their selection of fresh oysters, though the dog seems less impressed than the owners and patrons. Oysters both fresh and preserved were an ubiquitous part of the Victorian diet. Packed in barrels with ice and shipped fresh by express train or in tins they were available and popular all over the country.

The Montague Hardware Store.

The D. H. Bunbury store sold dry goods, groceries, and housewares. It is often referred to in old letters and diaries of the c. 1900 era.

TYLER REFRIGERATION

In 1927, the Tyler Sales-Fixture Company was founded by Jerry Tyler, his wife, and two employees in Muskegon Heights, Michigan. Their focus was on refrigerated display cases designed to help food merchants, restaurant operators, and others to sell food.

In 1937, after the purchase of the Dry-Kold property (Dry-Kold had been a maker of ice-boxes) in Niles, the firm relocated and changed its name to Tyler Fixture Corporation. After the tragic deaths of Jerry Tyler, his wife, and son in a Chicago hotel fire, Robert Tyler, Sr. became the president of the company. By 1953, Tyler Fixture Company was changed to Tyler Refrigeration Company.

Jerry Tyler, founder of Tyler Refrigeration Company.

Tyler Refrigeration was the first in commercial refrigeration to use welded steel construction, to introduce assembly line methods of manufacturing, to produce walk-in cooler rooms, and to introduce self-service frozen food display cases for retail stores.

Tyler's, like most of the Niles industries, was very involved with the life of the community. Company sponsored sports teams and social events like company picnics and outings were both common and popular. This c.1947 photo was snapped at the company picnic softball game. Bob Tyler, company president, massages a sore leg as the main office team is "getting the heck shellacked out of it" as reported by the company newsletter.

188

In 1936 or '37 the City Dairy staff posed for this group photo, showing both the old and the new.

THE CITY DAIRY

In the years before the invention of household refrigeration, a commonplace sight in the early morning was the milkman and his wagon making deliveries to each house in town. One of the changes in the middle years of the century that was easily noticed by the average person was the switch from horse-drawn to motorized milk delivery wagons.

In the 1930's, the City Dairy (one of several in Niles) made the change. Shown here are photos of the old and the new from a company scrapbook which documented the transition.

Above: Andy Anderson is ready to make his morning rounds in the early years. In the final years of horse-drawn wagons, rubber tired wheels were used to keep from awakening the neighborhood.

Probably taken during the transition, this man is proudly posing with the new City Dairy truck (complete with a phone number).

OLD KENT BANK-SOUTHWEST

Old Kent Bank-Southwest opened as the First National Bank of Niles on August 21, 1933. FNB of Niles was located at the present main office site on the south side of Main Street between Second and Third streets. This location had housed the Niles City Bank and City National Bank & Trust since July 3, 1901.

Mr. P. S. (Pat) Farquhar served as president and head of operations of the FNB of Niles until his retirement in 1955. During Mr. Farquhar's 22-year tenure, the bank was managed very conservatively, as were most area banks in the post Depression era. The only expansion of the bank from 1933-1955 occurred in 1945 when the FNB of Niles acquired the assets of the State Bank of Niles which had ceased operations.

In 1956, Samuel G. (Sam) Creden was named president and brought to the bank a new philosophy of growth. Between 1956 and 1972, the bank added eight branches in Niles, Barron Lake, Sodus and Benton Harbor and acquired banks in Berrien Springs and Dowagiac. In addition, the main office was expanded and extensively remodeled and a 20,000 square foot Operations Center built to house the staff required to support the rapidly expanding customer services. The name of the bank was also changed to the First National Bank of Southwestern Michigan to more accurately reflect the market and customers served. When Sam Creden retired in 1972, the bank had grown from a $13 million local bank to the largest bank in southwestern Michigan with deposits of $87 million and loans of nearly $60 million.

The bank continued to grow through the 1970's adding two more branches in the Benton Harbor – St. Joseph area and a subsidiary bank in Cassopolis. The late '70's also brought another name change as the bank's holding company, Western Michigan Corporation, merged with Pacesetter Financial Corporation. The First National Bank of Southwestern Michigan became known as Pacesetter Bank & Trust – Southwest in 1979.

In 1984, Pacesetter Financial Corporation was purchased by Old Kent Financial Corporation and the bank acquired its current name, Old Kent Bank-Southwest.

In the second half of the 1980's, Old Kent Bank-Southwest experienced a period of redefining its market by consolidating three offices, adding two branches through acquisition, and opening a new office in downtown St. Joseph.

The 1990's began with the construction of a new full service branch in Buchanan, reflecting Old Kent Bank-Southwest's continued commitment to serve the needs of its customers in Berrien and Cass counties. Banking services are currently being provided at 16 convenient locations throughout southwestern Michigan.

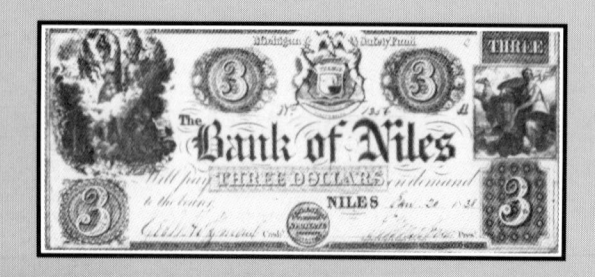

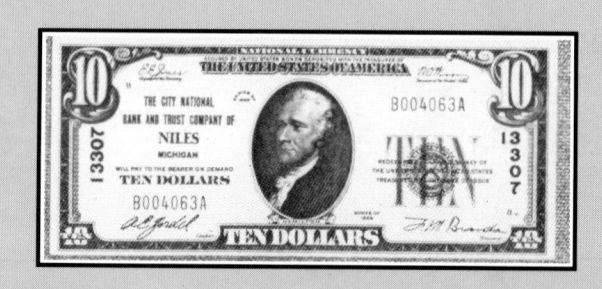

In 1901, Niles City Bank was located on the south side of Main Street between Second and Third streets. The main offices of Old Kent Bank-Southwest are now located there.

This 1951 photo shows the employees of the First National Bank of Niles, forerunner of Old Kent Bank-Southwest.

First National Bank's main office building, located on the south side of Main Street between Second and Third streets.

Old Kent's 20,000 square-foot Operations Center is located at Terminal Road and Industrial Drive. The Operations Center houses deposit services, finance & control and the proof department.

Personalities

Russ Thomas was a colorful and popular figure in Niles in the late 1940's and early 1950's. He promoted, built, and operated the Thomas Stadium which was located across the street from his family's restaurant, Thomas Drive-In. He served as mayor and was responsible for many civic improvements.

Don "Farmer" Marlin, spent 26 years as a professional wrestler on the national circuit starting right after World War II and retiring from the ring in 1965. He later owned a popular local "night-spot" and was active in local politics.

In 1961, Mayor Drew and his wife Eleanore (fourth and fifth from left), members of the city council, several department heads, and their wives, attended the Michigan Municipal League conference at the Grand Hotel on Mackinac Island.

Congressman E. L. Hamilton lived in a large home on the southeast corner of 6th and Broadway streets. The house is still standing as part of the Kling Apartment complex. In Congress he was the only man to hold the unique record of being "the father of three states;" having been involved in the introduction and enactment of the legislation for statehood of Oklahoma, Arizona, and New Mexico. He was best known here in his hometown for securing the "new" 1909 post office.

Niles has been home to many entertainers over the years but none have traveled more widely than Vic Hyde. With his "one-man-band" act, three-wheeled cars, and his steam calliope, Vic has toured the world as the "Honorary Mayor" of Niles for over half a century. Steam-engines had been a family interest and many will recall the steam tractors on his father's lawn on Grant Street.

Tommy "James" Jackson was a local musician who started with a band made up of young people from Niles High School. Known originally as "Tommy and the Tornados," they later changed their name to "Tommy James and the Shondells" and recorded a number of popular rock'n'roll songs. Their hit song *Hanky-Panky* was #1 on the Billboard list of "top 40" songs in 1966. They recorded it in the WNIL studios which were located on Sycamore Street.

193

Culture in Niles

There has always been an element of culture in Niles. In earlier times, the reading clubs sought to improve and maintain one's knowledge. Benevolent organizations such as the Women's Progressive League, and later the Niles Service League, have worked to encourage the growth and development of the arts and to assist those in need. The high school plays, concerts, musicals, art shows, and exhibits, are all examples of a continual flow of cultural events Niles has always made available to its citizens.

A child growing up in Niles has for many years had the opportunity (when affordable) of private dance, music, and art training. When the desired field of interest was not obtainable financially, the civic groups often have made scholarships available.

"One Hundred Years Ago."

DRAMATIC ENTERTAINMENT BY MEMBERS OF THE NILES HIGH SCHOOL,

THURSDAY EVE., MARCH 22, 1877.

REPUBLICAN PRINT.

This tintype photo is of an unidentified, but very early, Salvation Army officer from Niles. Since its beginning in the 1880's, the Salvation Army Church in Niles has served the needs of the community in a manner far above and beyond that of just a church organization.

This Niles High School music program is from 1877. Niles Public Schools have a long-standing tradition, that continues today, of offering quality drama and music to the entire community.

A 1929 club booklet from the Women's Progressive League which was started in 1912 by Mrs. W. W. Dresden, who was its first president.

A 1901 photograph of the ladies of the Seepewa Reading Club of Niles. The group is still active as a reading club and seeks to improve its members knowledge through reading. Clubs like this continue to take an active role in the community's cultural life.

The "Winter House" at Fernwood Nature Center was home to the founders of Fernwood Inc., Walter and Kay Boydston. As an historic site, the "Winter House" serves as a reminder of the early environmental, educational, and cultural contributions Kay Boydston made to the Niles area.
To quote from their own publication, the purpose of Fernwood is "to create a sense of environmental awareness and cultural appreciation." Its many programs include lectures and activities in various natural and environmental sciences, music, cultural history, and arts and crafts. These programs, as well as the botanical gardens and preserves, have attracted visitors from all over the world. In 1989 Fernwood celebrated 25 years with the dedication of the Mary L. Plym Visitor's Center (which contains the Kay Boydston Memorial Fern House). This new visitor's center is the most recent addition to the Fernwood complex.

Right: The Niles Theatre Group provided drama to Niles for almost 50 years. Shown in this 1938 photo from their production of *The Ghost Train,* are "Al" Pfister, Harold Klute, and Myrtle Lydick.

Below: The carriage house and boiler house of the H.A. Chapin mansion (the mansion itself had already been converted to use as city hall) was converted for use as a museum by the city and the W.P.A. in the 1930's. Prior to that the Fort Saint Joseph Historical Society, had operated the museum. It had been located in the Daily Star Building, courtesy of F. J. Plym, whose wife was one of the members of the society. The museum was able to open to the public in 1939 in its new city sponsored quarters. The museum became a part of the city's History Department in 1978. Its purpose is to collect, preserve, and exhibit, for public educational purposes, in a professional manner, the history and culture of the people of Niles.

195

ACKNOWLEDGEMENTS

Many members of the cummunity have contributed photographs, documents, research, services, and materials as well as time, interest and encouragement to this project.

Without their help this Tri-Centennial book would not have been possible. The authors would like to acknowledge their debt to those generous supporters. We hope that we have not inadvertantly omitted anyone. Unfortunately the size of the book did not allow all photos submitted to be utilized.

Alford, William Sr.
Amica, John
Armour, Dr. David – Mackinac Island Park Commission
Bainbridge, David – The Northern Indiana Historican Society
Barkman, Paul
Barnett, Dr. LeRoy – State of Michigan Archives
Beikman, Stan
Blackmun, Bill
Boyd, Michelle
Burge, Steve
Carmichael, Don – Four Flags Photo
Checchro, Janice
Clark, Ira & Barbara
Clymer, Elanore & Larry
Coffey, Janet
Cramer, Edward
Cuyler, Dave
Davis, Betty
Davis, Dorothy
DeLay, Norm
Dodd, Lee
Ducey, Jean
Edwards, Elanore P.

Erikson, John
Farmer, Betty
Ferguson, Lena
Fernwood Nature Center
Ferris, Martha Young
Florek, Zora
Fort Saint Joseph Historical Association
Frucci, Edith
Goodhand, Adah
Hahn, Leslie
Harrison, Robert
Heldman, Dr. Don – Mackinac Island Park Commission
Hillyer, Augusta
Huffman, Dr. John
Irwin, Marcia
Jarvis, Star
Keck, Louis
Leer, Rowena
Leidy, Fred
Lemke, Debbie
Lepel, Winnefred
Mann, Roger
Marazita, Paul
Marlin, Jacki
McCarthy, Marion
Moine, A. R.
Morse, Dave

Naser, Karen
Niles Public Schools
Niles Radio Shack, Data Communications
Noble, Richard
Old Kent Bank- Southwest
Olsen, Gordon – The Grand Rapids Public Library
Olsen, Kim
Palenchar, Ruth & Tony
Paterson, Ted & Harriet Family
Pawating Hospital
Peyser, Dr. Joseph L.
Potokar, Herman & Ruth
Potts, Leslie L., Sr.
Quick, Garold
Reeves, William
Reid, Samuel "Ted"
Ritchie, Paul
Rivers, Helen
Roberts, Jane
Rough, Dee
Sarratore, Joe
Shugars, C. E.
Slavecik, Margaret
Stephans, Eunice
Strayer, Virginia

Stethem, Lois
Swanstrom, Dave
Teske, Ed
Threlfall, Fred
Treesh, Harold
Vanderbeck, Andrew
Van Osdale, Bernie
Vosberg, Bruce
Waldron, Chuck
Walker, Irene
Whitfield, Phil & Marlene – Front Street Photo
Widder, Dr. Keith – Mackinac Island Park Commission
Wienke, Phena
Woodbridge, Robert
Wyburn, George
Zavitz, Mr. & Mrs. Greg

In addition an especial thanks is due to Old Kent Bank Southwest for their sponsorship of this publication and to the City of Niles for their contribution of the time and facilities for the writing.

196

RESOURCE & READING LIST

In preparing this book we have used a wide number and variety of resources, from published books, old newspapers, private scrapbooks and oral histories, to the anecdotal information written on the backs of old photographs. For those who would wish more in depth information we would suggest the following as a resource list on the history of Niles. While some of these books are available on the open market others are out of print. Most if not all of these works are available at or through the Niles Community Library. In addition to the published books, articles have from time to time been published in various scholarly journals which deal with aspects of our local history.

There are a number of books available (including some currently being promoted) which fail to measure up to professional standards of historical research. These books contain either outdated research, erroneous or fallacious reasoning, or are written to capitalize on an uninformed readership. We have avoided them in our research.

The following list contains some of the books which we have used that are generally accessible to the public and which we judge to contain reasonably accurate and reliable information.

Reading list for Fort Saint Joseph and the Colonial period.:

Old Fort Saint Joseph, by Ralph Ballard. A general survey written in the 1940's fairly accurate but dated and not footnoted. Now out of print.

At The Crossroads, by Armour and Widder, published by the Mackinac Island Park Commission, 1976. The story of the Revolutionary War in the Great Lakes area. Mostly about the Michillimakinac area but contains a lot of information relevant to FSJ

Letters From New France, by Joseph L. Peyser— (available only through the Indiana University at South Bend bookstore). A class text compiled by Dr. Peyser for his IUSB classes on the French Colonial history of our area. Probably the most current publication available, it is based on translations of official French government correspondence made by Dr. Peyser for the City of Niles and his extensive collateral research.

Keepers of the Fire, by R. David Edmunds from University of Oklahoma Press. A revised edition of Dr. Edmunds Ph.D. dessertation on the history of the Potawatomi people.

The Pokagons, 1683-1983, by James A. Clifton, University Press of America. A history of the Potawatomi people emphasizing the Pokagon band. This book is a popularization of the historical data presented to the federal government as evidence in the quest for recognition of the Pokagon band as an official tribe. It contains documentary source material as well as tribal oral tradition and anecdotal information.

The Michigan Pioneer Collections: especialy Vols. 9, 10, 11, 19, et. al. Contains published transcriptions on British military and official correspondence of the 1760-1815 period. They also give a great deal of information, both direct and indirect, on FSJ during that period.

The Post of the St. Joseph River During the French Regime, by Dunning Idle. This is a Ph.D. thesis circa 1945. It is very good but is dependent on the source material available at that time.

The Atlas of Great Lakes Indian History, edited by Helen H. Tanner published by University of Oklahoma Press.

There will be a new volume by Dr. Peyser available soon (in early 1992 from the University of Illinois Press) which will provide a comprehensive overview of the Colonial era in this area. It contains much new material he has located and translated from the various archives in France.

Published materials on the later history of the Niles area are more difficult to locate. There are three large county histories published in the 1880-1910 period which are of value. While they do not have the benefit of modern research or academic standards they contain much material that is of interest to historians. They, of course, are long out of print and may best be located at a library.

A History of Berrien and Van Buren Co's, Michigan, published by D.W. Ensign & Co. Philadelphia 1880.

A Portrait and Biographical Record of Berrien and Cass Counties, Michigan, by Biographical Publishing Company, Chicago 1893.

A Twentieth Century History of Berrien County, edited by Judge O.W. Coolidge, publisher unknown, date approximately 1906-1910.

Among the many resources for the section on fashions are the following:

The Wonderful World of Ladies Fashions by Joseph J. Schroeder Jr., Follett Pub.

Victorian and Edwardian Fashion by Alison Gernsheim, Dover Pub.

The Evolution of Fashion, by Margaret Hamilton & Peter Buck, Hill and Bucknell Pub.

Another resource that would provide interesting reading would include *The Complete American Houswife* by Julianne Belote, published by the Nitty Gritty Press.

In addition to the above listed county histories we would add:

The Making of Michigan by ——Kesterbaum, Wayne State U. Press

The Michigan Reader series by Erdmans.

The Kawneer Story by Thomas Strich, published by the Kawneer Company.

The Civil War, a multi-volume series by Time/Life publications.

INDEX

12th Michigan Infantry 46
60th Royal American
    Regiment 16
Air Line railroad 55
Airport 164-165
Allouez, Jean-Claude 8, 50
Anderson, Andy 189
Anderson, Charles 113
Architecture in Niles 124
Askins, John 18,
Automobiles 160-163
Babbitt Lumber Co. 186
Babcock, Fred 161
Ballard, Ralph & Mary 28
Banks 178-179
Barron Lake 58, 65, 72-73,
    116-117
Barron, Clem 80
Baughman, John 155
Beeson, Lewis 24
Bennett, Thomas 21
Bertrand village 50, 55
Bertrand, Joseph 23, 31
Bertrand, Madeline 31
Big Four Railroad 55, 56, 59
Boats
    Griffin 8, 19
    John F. Porter 34
    May Graham 35-36
    Nettie June 36
    Welcome 18-19
Boats, keel/flat 31, 34
Bond House 132
Bond, Mary 92
Bonine, Dr. E.J. 48, 108
Bonine, Dr. Evan J. 108-109
Boydston, Walter and Kay
    195
Bridges 120-121
Bunbury Store 187
Burke, John 28
Burnette, William 23
Cain, Noah 47
Cappon, Rev. John 53
Carey, William 32
Carnegie Library 148
Carr, Dr. 82
Cary Mission 27, 31, 32, 33,
    37, 92

Castle Rest 82 and
    following
Champion, Ella 87
Chapin Mansion 158-59, 183,
Chapin, Henry & Charles
    40, 41, 158-159
Chevallier, Louis 13 and
    following
Churches
    Baptist 50
    Bertrand 53
    Episcopal 52
    EUB 54
    Evangelical Assoc. 54
    German Evangelical 51
    Grace United Meth. 54
    Methodist 51, 107
    Presbyterian 51
    St. Francis of Assissi 53
    St. Johns United 51
    St. Mary's Catholic 51
Cincinatti, Wabash &
    Michigan Railway 55
Citizens National Bank
    178-179
City Dairy 189-190
Civil War 46 and following,
Clark, George Rodgers 19
    and following,
Clark, Ira 163
Colby, G.A. 48, 83
Collins, Mrs. E.J. 95
Cook, Sheridan 28
Cottrel, Patty 174
Courtemanche, Augustine
    Legardeur de 9
Cousins, Jim 174
Crane, E.H. 24
Cruzat, Fransisco 22
Dams 36-37
Daughters of the American
    Revolution 27
De Quindre, Dagneau 21-22
de Villiers family 12
de Villiers-Louis Coulon 15
Deans Drugs 185
Delano, Fannie Suter 150
Delano, Jeppe 150

DePeyster, Arent Schuyler
    19 and following
Depot, MCRR 55 and
    following
Dodge, John & Horace 58,
    106-107
Downtown Niles 80-81,
    122-123
Dresden Family 82-83, 194
Drew, Mayor Mowitt &
    Eleanore 192
Dry-Kold Co. 188
du Sable, Jean Baptiste
    Point 21
Eastlake Terrace 58
Elijah Murray Wagon
    Works 151
Erie Canal 31
Evert, Janet 28
Fashions 68-79
Fernwood 195
Fire Department 140-142
First National Bank of
    Niles 179
Fisher's Bakery 184
Flora, George 176
Ford, President Gerald 67
Forler, George K. 62
Fort Desquesne 15
Fort Michillimakinac 9
Fort Necessity 15
Fort Pitt 17
Fort Sackville 19
Fort Saint Joseph 8-23
Four Flags Hotel 133
Francis, George "Dude" 157
French Paper Company 25,
    40, 41,
French Paper Mill 40 and
    following, 120
French, J.W. 40, 116
Galt House 132, 142
GAR (Grand Army of the
    Republic) 47
Garden City 55, 60-61,
Garden City Fan Co 110
George Washington 14 and
    following,
Gillette, John 28

Gipner John F. 180
Gipner, John 60-61
Globe Dining Hall 186
Greek Revival style 31, 81,
    124
Grey, Issac 144
Griffin, Eli 47
Griffin, Miss Jean 28
Hamelin, Jean Baptiste 22
Hamilton, E.L. 144, 193
Hamilton, Gov. "Hair-
    buyer" 19
Hamilton Store 80
Hanson, Dr. C.P. 160
Harrah, William 113
Hatfield, John 47
Heath Aircraft Company
    164
Hotels 131-133
Hyde, Vic 193
Ice houses 65
Indians
    Foxes 13
    Iroquois 8
    Miami 8
    Potawatomi 10 and
        following, 84
    Weesaw 33
    Topash 33
    Topinibe 33
    Pokagon Band 33
Interurban Railway 134-139
Ives, E.B. 86
J & E Woodruff Store 186
James, Tommy 176, 193
Jerome, G.H. 86
Jesuit Missionaries 8, 50

Jumonville-Joseph Coulon
    de Villiers 15
Kawneer Co. 110-111, 181
Kemeny, Don 28
Kennedy Resort 116
King's 8th Regiment 20-21
Klute, Harold 195
La Salle 8
Lacey, Obed 144
Ladies Library Association
    148

Landon, Rufus W. 145
Lardner, Henry 145
Lardner, "Ring" 101-103, 151
LeBalme 21
LeClerc (LeClare) 23
Lombard, E. 24
Lydick, Mary 195
Malone, Peter 25
Mansfield, Harry 95
Marlin, Don "Farmer" 192
Mason, Dr. Phillip 28
McComber, James 48
McCoy, Rev. Issac & Christiana 32, 92
Medical/Hospital 82-85
Mell, M.Z. 161
"metis" 12, 31
Michigan Central Railroad (MCRR or MC) 55, 58, 60, 61, 67, 130, 139
Michigan Inn 131
Michigan Wood Pulp Company 40
Michigan Pioneer Society (collections) 24
Michigan Wood Pulp Company 39
Millard Family 83
Millard, Ted 180
Mills 36, 37
Montague Hardware 187
Moore, Steven 47,
Morris, Ella 87
Museum, Barron's 80
Museum, Fort Saint Joseph 195
National Printing and Engraving 162
National Standard Co. 113
New York Central Railraod (NYC) 59
Newman & Snell Bank 178
Niles "Blues" 171
Niles Board & Paper Company 40, 41
Niles Opera House 150
Niles Public Library 148-149
Niles School of Aviation 164
Niles Theatre Group 195

Niles, Hezekiah 31,
Noble Pontiac 162
Noble, Kate 87
Ohio Company 14
Ohio Paper Company 39, 40, 41
Old Kent Bank-Southwest 178-79, 190-191
Orphan Train 87
Ostrander, Lloyd store 167
Paine Bank 178-179
Paine, Rodney C. 178
Parades 88-90
Parc aux vaches 23
Paris Candy Store 184
Parker, Bascom 47, 101, 160
Pawating Hospital 82-85
Peak Family 150-151
Pfister, Al 195
Phillips, Rev. Joseph F. 54
Pike House 132
Plym, Mary L. 195
Plym, Mr. Francis J. 82, 110-111, 148, 195
Plym, Mrs. F.J. 28, 82, 195
Pokagon, Leopold 33
Police Department 156-157
Pontiac 17-18
Post Office 144-146
poteaux en terre 9
Pourre, Eugene 22
Ready Theatre 155
Ready, T.W. 155
Recreation and Leisure 114
Reddick, William 86, 104
River Saint Joseph 8-23
Riviera Theatre 155
Robbins, Robert A. 180
Robinson, D.D. 47
Robinson, Patty 176
Roeger's Candy Store 184
Salvation Army 194
Schlosser, Francis 16
Schmidt, Harry 151
Schmidt, F.C. 115
Schockley, Charles 145
Schockley, Rose Gitchell 145
Schools
    Ballard 96-97

Eastside 96-97
Ferry Street 96
First Assembly Christian 177
Northside 97
Ring Lardner 96-97
St. Mary's 53, 177
Southside 97
Westside Seventh-day Adventist 177
Union 92 and following
Seepeewa Reading Club 194
Sewing machines 49
Shankland, Mrs. Ruth 28
Simplicity Pattern Co. 112, 180
Sinclair, Patrick 20 and following
Slowey, Msgr. John 28,
Smith, Carmi 110, 111
Smith, Donovan 166
Smith, Dr. Willian H. 82
Smith, Hillis 24
Smith, Mrs. Hillis 28
Solloway, Capt. 157
Southern Michigan Railway 134-139
St. Louis (MO) 22
St. Louis Militia 22
St. Luke's "hospital" 85
St. Mary's Church 28
Sauk Trail 8, 20, 23, 84
Spanish Raid 22
Stowe, John 150, 151
Strand Theatre 155
Styers, Aleta 118-119
Theatres 155
Thomas, Russ 192
Threllfall, Fred 14
Troupes de la Marine 9, 12,
turtle soup 49
Tuttle, Joseph, 107
Tyler Refrigeration 181, 188
Tyler, Bob 188
Tyler, Jerry 164, 188
University of Michigan, Niles branch 93
Volant Mill 37
Voyageurs 10 and following
Walker III, Edward 180

Walling, Justice, & Lacey 30-31,
Ward, Mogomery 98-100
Weede, Ed. 176
Willard, Titus 92
Winslow, Dr. E. 82
Women's Progressive League 27, 194
Woodruff, D.O. 95
Wright, Hoel 47
WW I 91, 143
WW II 91, 180-181
Young's Dairy 104-105
Zanzibar 151
Zwergal, Phillip 156

OLD KENT BANK – SOUTHWEST

James A. Cousins,
Senior Vice President

James W. Giffin
President

Michael W. Stolz
Senior Vice President

Board of Directors

Murray C. Campbell

Robert D. Gottlieb

John J. Kinney, III

James E. Mack

William R. Racine

James F. Skalla

Taylor Tyler

Michele L. Boyd